OPPORTUNITIES and LIMITATIONS
in Religious Broadcasting

Edited by Peter Elvy

Published for
THE JERUSALEM TRUST
by the Centre for Theology and Public Issues,
New College, University of Edinburgh

First published in Great Britain in 1991 by
THE CENTRE FOR THEOLOGY AND PUBLIC ISSUES, NEW COLLEGE,
UNIVERSITY OF EDINBURGH
for THE JERUSALEM TRUST

ISBN   1 87012 615 7

Cover design: Joy Fitzsimmons
Origination: McCrimmon Publishing
Printed by: The Wolsey Press, Ipswich

CONTENTS

FOREWORD

The Reverend Professor Duncan B. Forrester

In a remarkable passage which is clearly autobiographical, the Danish nineteenth-century thinker Søren Kierkegaard tells of a child who is shown a series of pictures. Here is a knight on a charger; there is Napoleon, leading his troops to victory. Then comes a picture of a huntsman, dressed in green, his bow in his hand, staring ahead as he takes aim. That is William Tell. The story is told to the child; the Swiss hero is taking aim with consummate care, determined not to harm his beloved son, determined not to miss the apple.

In among the pictures which delight and instruct the child there is one that is different - the image of a man on a cross. This one will puzzle and disturb the child as much as the others delight him. He will be confused by this one, ugly picture among all the lovely ones, by the picture of a criminal among the pictures of heroes. He will ask questions. And as he listens to the story which is the answer to these questions he will find within himself a turmoil of conflicting emotions and a stream of questioning about who he is, and why this happened, and about the strange meaning of it all.

This tale of Kierkegaard's raises the issue of the sense in which Christianity - and religion - can "belong" in a powerful medium like broadcasting, which delights and instructs, and broadens horizons, and challenges. Can religious truth survive in a medium which amuses and advertises? Kierkegaard's answer, I am sure, would be that Christianity does indeed belong in that medium, rubbing shoulders with the other images and stories and amusements and instruction to be found there, like the picture of the crucifixion alongside the pictures of Napoleon and William Tell, and heroes rescuing damsels in distress. Its place is there, but it belongs there in a disjointed and disturbing way. It does not sit easily alongside much that is displayed in the box of delights. It is inherently different from a great deal of the other things that are to be found there. It belongs because it points to profundities of the human condition. It belongs because it claims to be true, to be public truth, open to inspection and examination, not simply the arbitrary choice of a declining minority group in our culture. It belongs because it is interesting and important. It belongs because it interacts, to confirm or question and be challenged by, much else that is on offer.

This, then, is an opportunity, and a responsibility, which should not be passed over - communicating truth to millions, and in the process of communication learning, clarifying and re-appropriating truth at a deeper level. And the limitations and dangers are no less real than the opportunities. Religious broadcasting can become frothy and amusing selling of religion that disturbs no one, challenges no one, and overlays truth with an impenetrable mass of candy floss. Or it can wallow in the nostalgia and razzmatazz of old-time religion, without any contemporary cutting edge. Or it can give way to the seductions of power and wealth, so that it can no longer proclaim good news to the poor, or show that God has chosen the weak to shame the strong. And yet good religious broadcasting - and there is a lot of it about - has a seriousness of content, presentation and impact which puts most traditional religious communication to shame.

The issues this book addresses are of the greatest moment. The editor and contributors bring a great wealth of experience and insight to bear on the opportunities, dangers and limitations facing religious broadcasting today. The initial purpose of this book is to serve as the resource document for the Jerusalem Trust's second Cranfield Conference. However, I am sure the book will also stimulate a widespread, vigorous and well-informed debate.

Duncan B. Forrester

PREFACE

Christian convictions about broadcasting are sometimes expressed with great force. *Opportunities and Limitations* is not intended to re-inforce one side of an argument. The book has been designed as a Speakers' Corner, with room enough for representatives from almost every point on the Christian compass. I record my thanks to twenty-five distinguished communicators from fourteen countries who have so cheerfully accepted this challenge.

For providing the opportunity and removing the limitations, I thank the Jerusalem Trust and its officers Hugh de Quetteville and Professor Roger Baker. The staff of the Centre for Theology and Public Issues of the University of Edinburgh have given me unfailing support and wise counsel.

I have received a great deal of help from Roland Pentecôte (Paris), Wolf-Dieter Kretschmer (Wetzlar) and Jim Gallagher (Brussels). They have become accustomed to my constant queries. Alan Hockley, former publisher of *The Lancet*, corrected the typescript and David Weaver read the book in draft form. I am indebted to both for their many criticisms and creative suggestions. For turning the draft into a book I thank Joan McCrimmon and Michael Shaw.

Peter Elvy

I

Albert van den Heuvel

The Three Futures of Christian Broadcasting[1]

What is the future of Europe?
What is the future of broadcasting in Europe?
What is the future of religion in Europe?

These are formidable questions and yet we shall have to come to terms with them before we can intelligently manage the discussion about the future of Christian broadcasting in our continent.

THE FUTURE OF EUROPE

The future of Europe lies in its unity. The turbulent developments of last year have shown that the process of unification has accelerated. Germany is the symbol. No longer do we have to hold agonizing discussions about the frontiers of the United States of Europe. It will include East and West, North and South.

European unity is built on economic presuppositions. It is not built on ethics or philosophy or culture. Even political unity follows-from-afar the emergence of one single market. The business community is pushing reluctant politicians. Cultural and even social developments are treated as derivatives, rather than leading aspects.

It is my conviction that these developments are irreversible as long as larger markets yield more profit and more affluence. It

9

was, after all, the desire for more consumer goods that mobilised the freedom-seeking people of Middle- and Eastern-Europe and it was the crippled economy of the East which lost it the cold war.

Therefore the many, many problems which still have to be overcome and which linger between our present situation and our future unity may slacken the process but will not stop it, let alone reverse it. Unification will go forward because of economic incentives. They will be gradually worked out in terms of political agreements, social and cultural forms.

There will be undoubtedly a long period of unrest and uncertainty, marked by nationalistic movements, attempts to resuscitate regional autonomy and a great number of exercises to revive minority cultures and customs. There will be heated debates, grim demonstrations, protests and even violence. Already now we are surrounded by such regrettable outbursts. Yet they are condemned to fail. Even the chaos in some East European countries should not fool us. They are warnings against power-structures holding nations and peoples away from European unity; they are, if you please, the result of economic mismanagement and forced unification. Even if countries like the USSR, Czechoslovakia and Yugoslavia disintegrate, their national subcultures will undoubtedly all join the struggle for European unity.

These counter-movements will undoubtedly stress the beauty of Europe's cultural diversity and condemn the artificial nature of economic unity. Yet, slowly and in spite of them, something of a pan-European culture will emerge. One of the European languages will become the new official *lingua franca*, even if a number of other languages will remain alive and keep developing.

None of us in this room will live long enough to see the final outcome of this process but most of us will see it emerge, slowly but securely. And more importantly, many of the decisions we now take and the positions we now accept will have considerable influence on the outcome and the shape of the European unity now being forged.

This means that we shall have to get accustomed to debates about broadcasting in which, as is already the case, the economic factor will heavily dominate the coming decades; in which political changes will be prepared in the marketplace and all cultural dreams will have to pass the test of financial and efficiency-oriented examination.

THE FUTURE OF BROADCASTING IN EUROPE

Broadcasting will be at the very heart of a uniting Europe just as it has already played a considerable role in bringing it about. TV and radio will accompany this process step-by-step, accelerating change and guarding diversity. In other words the role of broadcasting will be a double one. It will be on the one hand the strongest instrument to further unity and at the same time the best instrument with which to stay close to the people of the different regions in the new continent.

There will be many attempts at European programmes and - speaking for television - at European channels. It needs no great prophetic power to foretell that most, if not all, of these pan-European adventures will be commercially-operated, even if they accept a public service charge. The costs will be very high and no government or even group of governments will be able (or willing) to commit themselves without the financial commitment of those who see a possible profit in their functions.

I expect that pan-European channels will be replaced by continent-wide networks of TV channels, with one mother-organisation and a number of daughter-channels. Already a number of national broadcasting organisations are overrun by these new networks and I predict that we have not seen half of what is yet to come.

At the same time there will be another development. Side by side with continental networks there will be much emphasis on cultural diversity, on the defence and strengthening of different cultural heritages. The future of European broadcasting will be characterised by an emphasis on large-scale broadcasting and at the same time on programming close to the people. Broadcasting and narrowcasting will develop side by side. Belief in mass entertainment and mass information will go hand in hand with programmes designed for smaller target groups. Both commercial and public broadcasting will compete for the favours of target groups and special interest groups.

In short, we shall be confronted, in varying degrees, with a dual system in which commercial and public channels will compete bitterly. If public broadcasting does not change very quickly and very drastically the commercial channels will win out. If public broadcasting organisations do change, the two organisational forms will be complementary. Whether the public-broadcasting organisation will complement the commercial one or vice versa - a difference with great and deep consequences - cannot be foretold. That depends on the political decision-makers and ultimately on the quality of the programmes either has to offer.

In the coming years the number of channels and therefore the number of choices the public has will be probably greater than we now can imagine. These choices may well be between programmes which are quite similar, but may even be between the same type of productions. Choices will have to be made. And every time a channel is added, and puts on the same old programmes and more-of-the-same entertainment, audiences get smaller, revenues are again divided and the chances for quality programming to be seen by a large audience get dimmer. At this moment the dominant mood in Europe is to let the market decide who leads and who complements.

During the coming period huge sums of money will be spent on technological developments, which broadcasters may regard as secondary but which the European hardware industry regards as a priority. It follows from the one-sided dominant position of the economic model that hardware developers will have access to larger funds than programme makers. In order to fill the increasing number of new channels many trashy, cheap and doubtful programmes will be shown and they will probably find larger audiences than we would hope. Our only comfort lies in the knowledge that any system is capable of making beautiful productions since man's creative spirit can easily be hampered but will never be extinguished.

As far as our subject is concerned, every channel and every system will show religious programmes as long as a market for religion exists and as long as the true religious spirit produces quality. Of course there will be religious commercialism. There always has been. But there will be genuine probing in the

12

religious dimension of life. My educated guess is that there will be more religious trash and misuse of religion than pearls and gems of faith. But has that ever been different?

The Future of Religion in Europe

Of all preliminary questions, this one is the most baffling. The role of religion in the history of a divided Europe has been highly ambiguous. The ties between religion and secular power have been so strong that movements of change and renewal became almost automatically anti-religious. The tragic suspicion of science by the religious establishment led to a divorce between the scientific and the religious community. The alliance between the leaders of the industrial explosion and the leaders of the churches estranged the masses of the workers from the Christian churches. During the most atrocious regimes of the last decades a substantial part of Christendom lacked the courage to oppose their cruelty. On all these fronts the religious forces were defeated and humiliated: empty churches and abandoned religious institutions were the result.

Yet religion did not disappear. Closer observation shows that in all movements of reform, in the exploration of science and even in the emancipation of the masses of the workers, powerful (although often hidden) religious forces were at work. The loss of institutional strength restored the creative potential of the religious dimension and opened our eyes to the powerful and universal religious image of the community of faith as a rather small "serving household" within the human city: salt rather than earth, mustard-seed rather than harvest, light rather than the universe of darkness.

The question of the future of religion is the most baffling. Will this rowing-boat of recognised faith survive its own ocean of failure? Is it enough to point to a few renewers and prophets to proclaim the health of the whole? Will the growing unease about a society without an ethical base other than man's own feeble conscience lead to a resurgence of religion? Will the confusion of people in the face of scientific revolution, cultural upheaval and consumer greed be met by religious challenges? Or will our religion slowly slide into the dimly-lit rooms of our museums of cultural history and will man indeed live by bread alone? Who will answer these questions?

Returning to the future of Europe, we may assume one thing quite safely: growing European unity will create more religious diversity. Naive spirits may expect that secular unity produces religious unity as well; I assume that religion - and the arts -are the natural carriers for that other phenomenon we described: the need for cultural and personal identity in smaller units than a newly emerging continent can provide.

Protestants, Roman Catholics, Eastern-Orthodox traditions, all with their respective subdivisions, will keep a following alive since their great traditions cannot be stamped out as quickly as fashionable thinking predicted. The increasing mobility of people, the subsequent choice of religious alternatives and the influx of persons from less affluent nations will also increase the number of adherents of other religions in one-faith areas.

Whether any of these old or new religious communities will capture the imagination and the confidence of the masses, I do not know. Some of my agnostic and atheist friends are confident that all this moving around and all this change will quicken the process of secularisation and finally produce that independent personality on which they build their hopes. They may be right, but my expectation is that sooner or later the religious community will be once again the place where the discussion about questions which are basic to life will take place.

Ardent unbelievers, especially those who have cut the hawsers of the vessel of faith in which they were baptised and educated, will regard such a process as falling back into the dungeons of unfreedom. Maybe they are right. In the laboratory of faith no proofs exist. I have always held the conviction that in spite of the horrors of religious fanaticism, bigotry and pettiness there is no greater sign of human freedom than a person who, liberated from slavery and capable of taking his own decisions, chooses of his own free will to trust, serve and follow.

The future of religion in Europe unfolds in a landscape engineered by architects of the last generation. The basic questions of life - Who am I? Why am I? What is right? and What is wrong? What is to be trusted? and Is there hope? - were during their time often silenced by the noises of the merry-go-round of success and progress going on around and inside us.

One thing I do know: if Europe is to have a future at all, somewhere the basic questions will have to be asked. And where will they come up more naturally than in a community which claims a tradition of very basic answers? If Europe is to have a human future it must keep its best contribution to man's thinking and acting alive, namely its capacity to doubt inherited truths. And where is doubt taken more seriously than in a community of believers? The tradition of Socratic questioning, the protest of the Renaissance against medieval certainties, the fierce revolution of the Reformation against religious oppression, the proud tradition of the Enlightenment and the massive uprisings of social reformation all have their roots in the Judaeo-Christian faith; not in its established institutions but in its probing prophetic minorities.

More than the solid declarations of faith the movements of creative doubt have shaped the lands of this continent - and in them the future of religion is cast. Close reading of the basic texts of Europe's main religious movements shows that *questions-asked* had a more powerful influence than the *answers-provided*. Adam, where are you? Am I my brother's keeper? Why has the King turned away from the God of the Covenant? Why did the people erect a golden calf? Are you the one we expected or are we waiting for somebody else? Could you not wake and pray with me for one hour? Why hast Thou forsaken me? Why are you looking up at the heavens? Who is worthy to take the book of history - and break its seals?

The continuous and communal pondering of these questions has shaped the life of our lands and ultimately created the conditions for their unity. Perhaps this game of questions and answers will, once again, involve millions of people. Maybe the questions will only be raised and the answers discussed in the attics and cellars of society. It may involve a continent as in the time of the Reformation or a few house parties as in the time of the birth of the churches, but the discussion will not cease.

THE FUTURE OF CHRISTIAN BROADCASTING IN EUROPE

In a continent which has decided to build its future on economic presuppositions there will be preponderant interest in such programmes that appeal to those involved in that process.

15

Religion as a stabilising influence on society will be more popular than religion as a vehicle of protest and change. Mysticism will get higher votes on Wall Street than calls for social reformation. Most governments will rather hear calls to keep our national identity strong than attacks on social policies which try to cover up new forms of poverty and decline. I have never been much surprised or appalled by the emergence of televangelists in the USA. They present as fair an image of national values as do the fanatic Muslim leaders in Iran or the sedate Church of England in Great Britain.

In the first instance, religious communities will reveal the state of the nation, even if there are different signals as well. And religion - Christendom if you like - as the officially-recognised national religion cannot but support, translate and present the major values of the society in which it is so accepted.

In an economically-oriented Europe, commercial broadcasting will ignore religion as long as it is not regarded as a niche in the market. But as soon as religious needs arise, the commercial broadcaster will include it in his profit-oriented (consumer-oriented, he will say) package. In the US this type of religious broadcasting is a multi-billion operation and nobody will keep the merchant from peddling religion if it pays. They have done the same with entertainment and information. Any article in demand will help sell airtime.

Public broadcasting represents a very different approach to the media. It is not motivated by the profit-principle but by a desire to perform a public service. For that reason alone it will always strive to perform not an exclusive nor a complementary but a comprehensive function. It is motivated by the conviction to give the public the information it needs to function as an informed citizenry in a democratic society and to make the public aware of its cultural history and the fruits of new cultural developments; it will seek forms of entertainment offering recreation rather than relaxation and it will give viewers and listeners a chance to learn something they did not, or hardly, knew.

Of course, public broadcasters will do all of this in a way which serves as large a public as they can attract. That is even true for programmes directed at smaller target groups. To give a Dutch example: public broadcasters are proud that they produce programmes for our migrant workers, but they want these programmes to be seen by all the people in whose language they broadcast and are continuously trying to reach the larger Dutch public as well.

Religious programmes in public broadcasting will be part of that quadruple service of information, recreation, culture and education. They will aim to give the best information about religious matters they can muster. They will not aim for a programme that is only meant for believers - that is contrary to their mission - but for the public as a whole. They will not preach (that is, they will not address people as potential or committed believers for that is the task of the pulpit) but they will try to reveal the meaning of faith for people's thinking and action. They will seek attention for the cultural and social implications of religious controversies and therefore not cover up such unpleasantness. They will not make propaganda for their own faith, because propaganda is the essential task of commercial broadcasting. In a uniting Europe the pluriformity of religious beliefs and communities makes this information more important than ever.

We shall not understand the ways of thinking and acting of our Eastern Orthodox, Roman Catholic, Protestant, Muslim, Hindu or Jewish fellow citizens, if we are not better informed of what makes them think and act as they do. Religious information should be the most important antidote to prejudice and racial bigotry.

Christian programmes will show the depth of their identity by the width of their scope. In a deep theological sense they will want to show the footprints of their God by the way they treat people of other faiths. The greater their efforts are to make the public understand what moves people of other faiths the more clearly do they testify to their faith in the universality of the love and grace of the One they claim to worship. Therefore information is the essence of Christian programmes in a public service broadcasting organisation.

The cultural task of public broadcasting can be very close to the heart of the Christian programme-maker. In cultural terms the Christian community has a tremendous heritage, universally accepted by all men alive: cathedrals, music, painting, ballet (the liturgy!). The wealth of this heritage is immense. When the European public is confronted with its cultural heritage, reminiscence of faith is everywhere. When new cultural developments are at stake, however, one gets a different impression. Modern art, whether it is film, theatre, painting or music, gives the impression that the high waves of secularisation have drowned the religious character of human creativity. Like so many other areas of life it seems that the arts have been wrested away from the fascination with the divine, so characteristic of earlier periods.

The human condition, its hopes and attacks of despair, its loneliness and its introspection, its quest for insight and meaning are dealt with in the confines of earthly existence. Explicitly Christian art remains in existence but its manifestations carry the smell of the marginal. Most Christian broadcasts reflect this development: in ancient hymns in the traditional liturgy, the cultural heritage is dominantly present but with few exceptions modern culture has not been allowed to illustrate the mysteries.

It seems to me that this situation calls for fresh and courageous thinking from those who are responsible for Christian programmes on radio and TV. Such reflections could start from the observation that the themes of culture have not changed very much. Certainly the eternal battles between obedience and disobedience, light and darkness, freedom and bondage, good and evil, domination and sacrificial service, between revenge and forgiveness are omnipresent. They are subject, however, to what theologians might call Consequent Incarnation. Christian teaching has always held that the good news is about one revolutionary event: God becoming man; invisible presence taking on vulnerable human form; the supernatural expressed in natural form.

Now, after centuries of concentrated teaching about this central event, we begin to see that the Incarnation is not only an event but a wider phenomenon. This discovery has two roots: the traditional religious symbols have suffered heavily from various forms of misuse - as has religious language - and the Christian faith itself culminates in the humanisation of the divine. God, Christian testimony insists, has not become a Christian, but simply a man.

These reflections are not as daring as they may sound. In the early Christian texts the Rabbi from Nazareth employs the parable to portray the mysteries of the Kingdom he announces. Seemingly simple stories, vignettes of life are the ultimate form used to reveal the message. It baffled his students and irritated the religious leaders of his day. The crowds, however, confused and directionless as crowds tend to be, recognised this form of revelation and even experienced it as authoritative. In the parables God is absent and yet very present. He plays a leading role in them, but always in disguise. Parables are the ultimate expression of the Incarnation; God has become man, not only in the person of Jesus of Nazareth as tradition has emphatically proclaimed, but also in the form of righteous judge, the father of the prodigal son, the good Samaritan, the sowing farmer, the courageous and reliable shepherd.

Parables do not demand exclusiveness. They function among myriads of other stories. They are not more beautiful, more powerful or more attractive than other human parables which carry a different and maybe opposite meaning. They are thrown at the crowds so that people can choose their model of life. The listener is free to choose for or against them. They are free to choose from injustice, compromise, wealth, revenge, coward-ice, self-protection. The New Testament tells us that man's freedom goes so far as to include the murder of God's own son. In his choices man reveals from where he takes his inspiration. Tragedy occurs when man is not aware of his freedom to choose and behaves as a slave of fate. Parables are used in the gospels to illustrate man's freedom. He always has more than one choice. And the point of each parable is that man's choice for the lifestyle of the Covenant is always costly but also always deeply rewarding. So parables are an appeal to man's freedom and a salute to his ability to choose life!

One of the great challenges for "Christian broadcasting in a uniting Europe" is to tell The Story in terms of drama in which the Incarnation is taken seriously. This generation does not need the explanation of faith as much as the humanisation of life. Christian broadcasters can be satisfied when they can show explicit Christian drama. Most of their patrons, be it their bosses in broadcasting or the church's representatives, are reluctant to make funds free for such productions. I share their reluctance because I think that religion departments should indeed produce drama and other art forms, not the explicit Christian type. Religion is too precious to produce soap.

Explicitly Christian drama is trite. In trying to reveal the power of faith it usually covers it up. Explicit Christian art or culture mostly make the most serious mistake of the artistic trade; it does not celebrate the mystery but tries to solve it. It does not point to revelation but it does reveal. But faith, like miracles cannot be seen. It must remain ambiguous to keep its character. Self-evident faith is no faith. Proven miracles are propaganda. If Christian broadcasting would dare to show some forms of parable art, especially drama, by using either existing so-called secular theatre and film or if it could commission productions in which the great themes of the Christian tradition are mysteriously present, its future is very promising indeed. But if it continues to demystify the mystery and bluntly pretends to show the invisible, it will rightly disappear.

The same is true for music, painting, ballet and any other element of culture we are confronted with. Similar remarks could be made about entertainment. There is a silly debate going on whether public broadcasting should produce entertainment at all; the "commercials" are so much better at it! As if what usually goes for commercial entertainment is so inspiring! (I would much rather trust the profitmakers in the media with culture than with entertainment!) Or has entertainment lost its style-setting dimension? Have all distinctions between recreation and amusement disappeared?

Good entertainers, from Chaplin to Woody Allen, from Cliff Richard to the great mime artists of our time, have been much more influential than a whole generation of preachers and priests. Entertainment worthy of the name of re-creation, belongs to the heart of public broadcasting, and should be one of the cornerstones of Christian programmes. No Biblical jokes, please, no shady semi-funny colloquies, but recognisable parable humour.

Now once again, my plea would be that we take seriously what Bonhoeffer taught my generation so eloquently: there are more secular seeds which are sown in the heart of man than we are willing to admit. To make an allusion to an old English joke: A bishop is not a phenomenon. A good comedian is not a phenomenon, but a bishop yielding his airtime to a good comedian, that certainly is a phenomenon. It would create confusion, anger and amazement but the people would love it and understand.

In comedy, cabaret and satire there is always an element of the supernatural, or "the metanatural", if the former word has lost its natural flavour. Real humour transcends and we know its healing effects. We know how it makes criticism bearable and how it can be painfully revealing. Above all, it communicates better than most other signals between people. Let the comedians be commissioned by the churches to write a few programmes about the heavy burdens we all bear; and let the churches be courageous enough to put on the air what already exists and what they recognise as concomitant with their message.

Europe has a future, broadcasting has two futures (commercial and public); religion has three futures (a commercial one, a service one, and one we do not control at all!). Christian programmes have a future if they give up propaganda and the smell of omniscience and learn to ask the best metanaturalists we have to do their thing in church-time. Let them commission, not our best known Christians to write Christian programmes, but our best people to write those programmes that broadcasting executives do not dare to put on the air.

Albert H. van den Heuvel has held major offices in the World Council of Churches as well as in Dutch politics. Dr. van den Heuvel is minister-emeritus of the Netherlands Reformed Church and is now vice-Chairman of the Board of the Dutch Broadcasting Corporation.

II

Jaan Kiivit

The New Religious Situation in Eastern Europe[2]

After more than twenty years I was able to visit Germany again. It was just at the time of the reunification and *Der Spiegel* came out with the headline: UNITED BUT STRANGERS - THE DISSIMILAR GERMANS. It dealt with the question of whether the Germans, after forty years of going their separate ways, would be able to become one nation: The differences in mentality and life-style are noticeable; it is impossible to become one people without difficulties; the East Germans behave like second-class Germans and are treated that way too.

It came as no surprise to me that there is a character variation between the Germans. But, coming as an observer from Estonia, a country which has been occupied by the Soviet Union since 1940, this was also my feeling: We Baltic people, we Estonians, Latvians and Lithuanians, are in comparison third-class beings. But at the same time, I thought, things could be worse. There are fourth-class beings in the neighbourhood. These are people who have lived even longer under the Soviet regime. Above all, I thought of the national minorities in the Soviet Union and among them especially I thought of my Lutheran brothers and sisters, of the peoples with Finnish origins and of Germans. In comparison with them the three Baltic national groups are better off in all respects.

Obviously the existence or lack of basic political rights is important. But our own experience, during the *perestroika* years, has uncovered a background symptom; the phenomenon of the "homo sovieticus", the deformation of the soul, the change in personality structures in the citizen's state. Perhaps historians will some day say that this symptom of degeneration was the greatest "achievement" of the Communist Regime. To me it seems that people, indoctrinated by the state and whose minds were constantly made up for them by the state, pose the greatest problem to a post-Communist society in a time of new departures.

We must never forget this human factor when judging the political or religious situation in Eastern Europe. By forcing the citizens to conform to their own way of thinking, the Communists have educated them to hypocrisy and subsequently harmed them psychologically. The totalitarian power of the state was secured by an elaborate system of surveillance, spying, intimidation and punishment. A Communist system can only be maintained as a police state.

Nowadays the previously anti-clerical position of the state's policy towards the church has changed. The laws restricting religious activities have been lifted and the relationship between church and state has been re-established on a more liberal basis. In order to illustrate this drastic change and make its meaning more comprehensible, I will take a look back. I will use as an example the fate of the Estonian Church under the Communists' rule but all the other churches in Eastern Europe have suffered in the same fundamental way.

Denominationally Estonia is Lutheran. During the time of national independence (1918-1940), 80% of the population belonged to the Lutheran National Church, about 17% were Orthodox Christians and the rest belonged to Free Churches. The occupation of Estonia by the Soviet Union marked a turning point in the life of both the country and the church. The legal enforcement of Soviet law was automatically applied in Estonia. For the churches that meant that any children's work or youth work, any publishing and missionary work was forbidden. The property of the church was secularised and the theological faculties were closed. Socially, pastors and parish workers were classified as second-class citizens. The Lutheran church was deprived of its financial support, its faculty for educating future generations and its function in society itself. Already in the 1940s - due to deportations, arrests and emigration - the church had lost more than two thirds of its ministers. Today it has never really recovered from this haemorrhage. Other churches and religious communities are no better off.

As a result of decades of massive atheist propaganda and repression Estonian Christianity has lost its spiritual and cultural influence. The church was pushed into a ghetto outside society. During the last forty years the activities of parishes have been restricted almost entirely to a weekly service on Sunday and the occasional special duty. Only people who had nothing to lose dared to go to church - pensioners, workers and officials who were not open to bribes. Before 1988, less than 10% of Estonians publicly confessed their Christian belief. Also, because of the forced integration of Russians, the proportion of Estonians within the entire population has sunk to 60%. Meanwhile two generations have grown up indoctrinated by atheism. In a religious sense they are illiterate or even prejudiced.

The church adjusted to this pressure and was forced into line. How the mechanism of being forced into line was handled has not yet been uncovered. In the former GDR the Stasi past is now being cleared away. But the Baltic states and Baltic churches are not yet ready for such a step. The old guard is often still riding in the saddle. Perhaps it will take years to find out how the church survived at all during the Communist dictatorship. At present it is impossible to grasp the effects that this horrible regime has had on the church.

However one can already say something. On the parish level the infrastructure was destroyed completely and outsiders were prevented from joining. Because the life in the parish had shrunk to such a terrible extent, all parish duties were executed by the pastor alone or with the help of his wife. Gradually the church consisted merely of pastors. At the same time the Christian responsibility of the laity, that each parish member is responsible for the house of God, died out.

The normal running of the government or church was hampered by surveillance and interference by the bureaucracy of the state. The supervision of the church was handed over to an official ecclesiastical department, which was itself working as a branch of the national security office and the ideological department of the Central Committee of the Communist Party. The government of the church was compiled from a list put forward by the offices of the state and was formally accepted by the synod. In this way the leadership of the church was in the hands of men behaving loyally towards the atheist state. One can imagine the extent of distrust that this caused within the church.

Honest and dishonest people in the government of the church was not the only problem. The fact that two opposing attitudes were working together within the church was the real concern. One side hoped that the church while being forced to work with the Communist regime might still retain a tiny space to preach the Gospel and preserve the church's life within society; the other side suggested that the church by co-operating with the Communist regime and consequently with the national security system (the cornerstone of the totalitarian regime) loses its soul. Everyone was involved in the system (differing from each other only by degree and the extent of their involvement). In my experience, I can say sadly that the people who chose the first way have somehow lost their integrity. They were corrupted, as the system they worked with was in itself corrupt.

Jaan Kiivit is a pastor of the Estonian Evangelical Lutheran Church. His parish is in the Estonian capital Tallinn. His late father (also named Jaan Kiivit) was a distinguished Archbishop of Tallinn.

III

László Lukács

From Buzz to Satellites

1989 will certainly be the title of a new chapter in the future history books of Central and Eastern Europe. Forty years of foreign occupation, of totalitarian dictatorship, of a party-state with atheism as the official ideology came to an end in 1989. Those who are living (or surviving) participants of these historical changes can still hardly believe their eyes. Are we really free? What are the new possibilities of freedom? What are the new opportunities - the new challenges - the new dangers?

The changes in Hungary have had far-reaching consequences in the field of the media. A free press is essential to the maintenance of a free democracy. In our country the press also had the task of helping to create democracy: struggling for its own freedom to tell the truth, the simple truth about our present and about our past and thus destroying the network of lies imposed on society. The media today are free, completely free. Indeed there is no valid law about the press and according to some liberals there is no need for any regulation. Media freedom can lead to irresponsibility or manipulation, to the violation of the human rights of private persons or of ethical values. The limits and the price of freedom can also be seen here for freedom can never mean that anybody is free to say anything. The media have a duty to tell the truth, to defend the truth, to serve the dignity and rights of human beings and the common good of society.

The churches, too, discover themselves in a new society of complete freedom. Up till now they struggled, wisely or unwisely, courageously or with compromises, against a totalitarian system, against the suppression of religion. Now they find themselves in an open pluralistic society. They are trying to find their bearings in the new social environment. They are learning the importance of the media which may be hostile savages menacing the integrity of the church but may also be useful servants in the task of evangelization.

1988 is a landmark in the life of the media. As far as the press was concerned, only publications authorised by the government had the right to exist. In practical terms this meant that the Roman Catholic Church - which accounts for two thirds of the population - could publish one quarterly, one monthly, one weekly and one news-agency bulletin. The Protestants had proportionately less publications. On radio, 25 minutes was provided for all the churches every Sunday. Again, this time was distributed proportionately according to the number of adherents. The Catholics had 18 Sunday-programmes a year. Censorship was more than routine: the sermon, delivered in a Mass-imitating ceremony, had to be submitted to the authorities weeks before. Television was a no go area - no religious programmes were transmitted until 1989.

The only way to speak about religion was in and through culture. Literature, music and the arts served as a vehicle for transmitting religious ideas. Documentary films revealed the recent past of Hungarian history. Truth slowly prevailed over lies and ignorance.

The quiet revolution of Hungary had immediate results in the field of communication. In 1989, a new bill was issued. Any citizen now has the right to publish any kind of newspaper. A new springtime arrived for the printed media; former *samizdat* publications became official, dozens of new publications (weeklies and monthlies) were published. At the moment, the total amount of new publications exceeds three hundred.

The new freedom has cast its shadows too. Freedom of expression is now limited by the severe and relentless rules of economic life. While new periodicals are published, others die away. Many a publication fades away in its infancy - after just a couple of issues. The free market system does not necessarily favour quality. The tabloid newspapers have the greatest profits. Sex and pornography is sold in any quantity, fulfilling the lowest desires of the crowd.

There are a dozen or more new Catholic publications, from noble intellectual quarterlies to parish bulletins. One chronic disease is diagnosed everywhere: there are hardly any good Catholic journalists with proper training and experience. Most of the new editors are well-intentioned amateurs with much enthusiasm and imagination. But these qualities cannot always help, without proper skills and education, infrastructure and money.

Broadcasting, on the other hand, reacted in a different way to the political changes. Hungarian state television has two channels and neither of them are commercial. Hungarian Radio has three channels. An important fact of life is that there is a moratorium on the allocation of frequencies. Three commercial channels have started to operate in the recent past - but the moratorium is a type of insurmountable Chinese wall in the way of the dozens of applicants for a commercial radio or television programme. All this takes no account of the different local cable-television systems which have a growing importance.

Coming to our particular topic: religious broadcasting. There has been an ongoing war in the last three years. It is very similar to a water-polo match. It seems to be an innocent sport with fair rules and fair players but in reality the risk and the price of victory is great. The basic question is: Have the churches the right to broadcast on national radio and television as masters of their message? (We may call this function evangelization or the fulfilling of a prophetic role in our society). Or are the churches the mere objects of various programmes, produced by others. Has the church the right to appear in communication as a major group in a democratic society? Or is the church a private association? Anyone can report about them, or they can buy some transmission time on a commercial basis.

The European tradition favours the first solution. In a democratic society, the church should have the right to announce its message through the national media, because a significant part of the society belongs to them. Others make claims for the American liberal way. The churches are private associations. They can have their own stations and channels, or buy as much time as they want - as can any single person or social group in a free society.

Let us look at the history in brief. Christmas 1988. Fresh winds of democracy foreshadow a new interpretation of liberty. West Germans place an order for the live transmission of the midnight Mass from the Coronation Church in Budapest and they are ready to pay for it. Money counts: the Mass is transmitted. There are rapid negotiations. It would be scandalous and also uneconomical, if the Mass is only transmitted abroad, and not at the same time in Hungary. At the last minute the decision is made. The Christmas midnight Mass was transmitted for the first time in the history of Hungarian television.

November 1989. Negotiations between the President of State Television and the representatives of the churches. There is a gentleman's agreement. The Roman Catholic Church receives 25 minutes' broadcasting-time per week. The churches belonging to the Ecumenical Council receive 15 minutes. The Jewish community receives proportionately less. In addition, there is agreement for ecumenical programmes on a monthly basis.

The programmes started in May 1991. The Roman Catholic programmes consist of a 10-minute Catholic News Chronicle, 5 minutes for Children's catechesis, 5 minutes for Questions of Christian living and a 5-minute Bible commentary. The monthly ecumenical programme is a 30-minute ecumenical round table once a month. Six or seven times a year there are programmes in a series entitled "Christian Witnesses". These are about the lives of outstanding personalities - a Hungarian Jesuit in Romania who spent 22 years in prison, a Benedictine priest, arrested in 1946, who spent 10 years in the Siberian Gulags.

As far as the structures are concerned, there is a Catholic section within Hungarian television - though it struggles daily because of the lack of equipment, money and experienced personnel. In Hungarian radio the structure has not changed. Last autumn the church protested. Why did the radical changes in the whole political system of Hungary not also have an effect on Hungarian radio? The first reaction was astonishment. Then came negotiations. Now there is a promise of a new structure, in which the churches will have the right to open their mouths. The deadline is October 1991.

Finally, a unique and courageous initiative or adventure deserves to be mentioned. Some enthusiastic Christian experts decided to found a religious broadcasting station on a commercial basis. The Roman Catholic, the Reformed and the Lutheran churches agreed and also the Jewish Community joined in the enterprise. Its name is Radio Pax. The aim is to transmit religious programmes with a great deal of music and features about art and literature. The only barrier to be overcome is the frequency moratorium. There is some hope for a solution in the course of the year. If they obtain a frequency, Radio Pax will call to all listeners, believers and non-believers, with the message of the Lord's revelation and will be a showplace for Jewish-Christian culture.

László Lukács was appointed director of the Media Centre for the Hungarian Catholic Bishops' Conference in 1984. Dr. Lukács has published more than two hundred articles and edited several books.

IV

Horst Marquardt

What Do I Mean by Evangelical Broadcasting?

Is it all about the Electronic Church, or fundamentalists wanting to draw attention to themselves, or the dogmatic voice of sectarians? Not one of these ideas is correct.

I am using the expression Evangelical broadcasting for radio missions like TransWorld Radio (TWR), the Far East Broadcasting Company (FEBC or FEBA), HCJB (Voice of the Andes) and ELWA. All over the world these stations take the gospel - in more than one hundred languages - to peoples and language-groups that can hardly be reached by churches or missions. I will restrict myself to the experiences of Evangeliums-Rundfunk (ERF) which happens to be the national partner of TWR in Germany. For ERF Evangelical broadcasting not only means the spreading of the gospel of Jesus Christ into areas which can be looked upon as traditional. It also means transmitting the Biblical message to people who may be confused by a wide spectrum of beliefs within pluralistic Protestant churches. ERF also strives to reach those who have lost their orientation in our increasingly secularized society.

Some of the arguments with which Evangelical broadcasting is repeatedly confronted are as follows:

First argument: Who listens to your broadcasts?

Answer: So many people that in the German headquarters of Evangeliums Rundfunk, for example, some 160 staff members are employed in order to cope with the work load. ERF Switzerland, near Zurich, has 20 and the branch in Nairobi 40 staff members.

According to an Emnid survey conducted in 1990, about 3.5 million Germans of the former Federal Republic are familiar with ERF. More than half of them listen to one or more broadcasts and some ten thousand indicate that they listen regularly. One set of examples from the ERF Department for Foreign Languages is particularly encouraging: The increasing mail in response to broadcasts beamed to the USSR increased from 1361 letters in 1988 to 3076 in 1989, to 4181 in 1990. In just the first four months of 1991 there were 1424 letters received.

Second argument: Medium and shortwave broadcasts are no longer attractive.

Answer: It is true that people in North America and in Western Europe prefer listening to FM. But nevertheless, for both TWR and ERF, transmissions via MW and SW are of high importance. The worldwide broadcasting of TWR is a great advantage. For instance, the USSR is being reached via SW from the TWR transmitter in Guam in the South Pacific as well as from the TWR transmitters in Monte Carlo. What these broadcasts mean for the countless citizens of the USSR is far beyond the estimation of people living in the so-called "free West". In the USSR we come into contact with scientists, artists, teachers and students who make known to us how valuable it is for them to listen to evangelistic broadcasts, especially since there is such a painful spiritual vacuum in their country. In highly populated areas of the USSR, individual Christian organisations are airing their programmes over the local FM stations. In this way a special few are privileged to receive Christian radio programmes in FM quality. But one look at the map of this huge land makes it quite obvious that in the near future it will be impossible to reach this vast population with an FM Christian voice.

In Central Europe - Germany, Switzerland, Austria - it is normal to listen to FM. Therefore, ERF has an agreement with about 35 FM transmitting stations to provide them with special evangelistic programmes. Every Sunday morning in Berlin, a two-hour live programme is broadcast via the most popular, private station.

AM (medium wave) programmes with an evangelical content are well accepted by many people in Central Europe in spite of the limited propagation conditions. This information was gathered through a listeners' survey according to which 50% of our regular listeners are tuning to the ERF evening broadcasts. 30% receive the morning broadcasts. Three times during the day a further ten thousand listeners are reached over shortwave.

Third argument: Are there not already enough Christian broadcasts for listeners in Germany and Switzerland?

Answer: Nearly all public and private stations are transmitting morning devotions, services and reports. In addition to this, there are news and information broadcasts about the Christian world as well as on special Christian topics. This provides the explanation about why such a large number of people still listen to ERF's broadcasts: Evangelical broadcasting deals with topics which are not dealt with otherwise.

Fourth argument: Only pious people are listening.

Answer. Believers need direction, correction and encouragement as much as other people. The parents of a Downs Syndrome child living near the city of Trier made the following statement: "Through your broadcasts we found new life in Jesus Christ. We are now more thankful and realise that our child brings us more blessings than burdens."

The Chairman of the EKD (Protestant Church in Germany), Bishop M. Kruse, has stated that it is the important topic of the churches to tell the people "how to become a Christian" but also to tell the believer "how to remain a Christian". Public stations in Germany and Switzerland occupy themselves very little with this topic. In numerous variations, ERF takes it up again and again.

Fifth argument: Non-believers are not being reached.

Answer: This is not true. About 10% of the regular listeners indicate that they tuned in by accident. Another 50% became listeners through the recommendation of others. Among these there are many who were or are non-churchgoers or non-believers. One letter puts it well: "Your broadcasts sound quite different from what we hear in church. If there were a church sermon like this in church, I would attend the service more often."

Sixth argument: The programme-format is outdated.

In general, this comment cannot be justified. There may still be some unteachable producers who continue to offer their sandwich-type programme. They put their sermons between songs and announcements. This concept, although originally developed for North America, is sometimes offered to listeners in the differing cultures of Eastern Europe, Asia and Africa. This might not be the best method to proclaim the Gospel. ERF, however, was concerned from its beginning to use every possible programme format, from documentaries, reports, interviews and dramas to mixed musical broadcasts. ERF has a studio choir as well as its own orchestra. Many young German songwriters were discovered by ERF.

Seventh argument: Radio mission work is too expensive.

Answer: Of course it would be ideal if the big stations (like ARD and ZDF in Germany and SRG in Switzerland) would make air time available. However, the legal situation alone does not allow this. Thus Evangelical broadcasting has no choice but to purchase air time. A 30-minute evening broadcast over medium wave Monte Carlo costs nearly DM 25,000, and a 30-minute TV broadcast over Super Channel costs DM 11,100. However, if you take into account that after a 30-minute TV programme there are viewer-reactions from Scandinavia, Central Europe and Turkey, you know at least that the money was well-invested.

And there is a whole undertaking that needs to be financed - the workers, the building, the vehicles, machines, the telephone charge and the postage. Under German law, the church has a right to collect tax. The listeners who help finance our programmes are mostly those who pay the church tax. They pay their radio licence fees as well. It is remarkable that they not only finance our broadcasts in their own language. They also give financial support for broadcasts in other languages like Armenian, Kurdish, Russian or Turkish.

Eighth argument: Evangelical broadcasting competes with the churches.

Answer: The case here is just the opposite. ERF, for instance, supports the work of all Protestant denominations. ERF sees itself as an extension of the Body of Christ. The 13 staff members of the ERF Counselling Department are in contact with 1800 voluntary helpers from all parts of Germany, Switzerland and Austria. The aim of Christian counselling remains always the same; to encourage the person who receives counselling to stay in his church or to join a church.

However, conflicts cannot be avoided where a living faith is being hindered or even killed by mere Christian tradition. Some parishes and pastors are upset by the testimony of a new believer. But this only comes about if you yourself no longer see the necessity for being converted and reborn as a vital part of your preaching and of your personal faith.

Ninth argument: There is no such thing as Evangelical broadcasting, there is only broadcasting.

Answer: This is true. There are no "Christian" transmitters and actually no "Christian" transmissions. Therefore there is no Evangelical broadcasting. However, there are Christians, in this case evangelical Christians who are answerable to God and men, who make use of radio and TV as a means of mass communication to proclaim the will and the Word of God. Evangelical broadcasting means to make plain by the means of radio and TV that all people can find meaning for their lives in Jesus Christ. In the mass media these topics are rarely dealt with and are presented in a very subdued manner. Therefore Evangelical broadcasters have to proclaim this truth more explicitly.

Horst Marquardt worked as a radio-journalist in the former Soviet-occupied East Germany. A Communist, he found Christ whilst reading the Bible. In 1960 he felt called to establish Evangeliums-Rundfunk in Wetzlar.

V

Bill Thatcher

What Have You Done for Me Lately?

Public Service Broadcasting is not easily defined. A United States Supreme Court Justice, speaking about pornography, once said that he didn't know how to define it but he knew it when he saw it. The same comment could be made about Public Service Broadcasting. It wasn't all that long ago that a European viewer or listener at least knew where to tune to receive it - even if they couldn't define it! Now even tuning to it can prove as challenging as defining it.

What is PSB? Is it a system, a programme, or a programme-style dependent on a system? Or is it a system dependent on a programme style? Who determines what comes under its purview? Is there some group of enlightened ones setting its agenda? How is the success of PSB measured? Is the measurement objective, subjective or a mixture of both? If there is measurement, who does it? Who controls PSB? Can the words public service be used with broadcasting without the term becoming an oxymoron? Is there general agreement on the answers to any of these questions?

Who says it's a Bird?

Many people have tried to define Public Service Broadcasting. A most thorough attempt at definition of PSB in the UK was made in 1986. It can be found in a booklet by the Broadcast Research Unit entitled: *The Public Service Idea in British*

Broadcasting: Main Principles[3]. But advertisers and others have strongly disputed this description. Along with other attempts at definition of PSB, some create additional problems for public service broadcasters by arguing *from* conclusions rather than *toward* conclusions. There is a sense of transitory value in PSB when arguments for its continuance are based upon present activity.

And a *universal* definition has certainly eluded the grasp of a host of searchers. Any person still searching is as doomed to failure as the Greek philosopher Diogenes was in his search for an honest man. The very nature of PSB, so deeply rooted in the particulars of society, makes its definition necessarily parochial and ever-changing - even within Europe. It also means that there is no "right way" of public service broadcasting waiting to be exported round the world.

In the debate and discussion swirling around PSB today, some measurement standards applied to PSB by both defenders and detractors reflect spurious assumptions. It is somewhat like the man asked to answer yes or no to the question, "Have you stopped beating your wife?" when he never beat her in the first place. There is no way to answer and be understood because of the underlying assumption.

Subjective terms of description for a PSB structure assume a uniqueness of purpose anchored in the obligations of public service. But public service must apply to all elements in the broadcasting system for PSB to work well. The complete rationale for PSB hinges upon such matters as indigenous productions that celebrate our cultural uniqueness, greater minority access, quality production or unbiased, investigative reporting. This is shaken when a *Jewel In The Crown*-type film is produced by a commercial television company or a cable company provides a channel for minority programming. If others are doing it why do we need a PSB structure?

Equally puzzling is why public service broadcasters allow success to be redefined for them in either market share or economic categories. When the government has raised the issue of consumer choice, PSB has not known how to respond. It's like an ornithologist moving some birds out of their classification as birds because these birds cannot fly, while ignoring other fundamental birdlike characteristics. Measurement standards are only useful when 1) ascribed by a recognised authority and 2) there is an understanding of what is to be measured, whether a bird or a broadcasting system. PSB is an important expression in the broadcasting of a democratic society because its purpose is social not economic.

Considering the difficulty in defining PSB, many broadcasters have taken for granted the ideal of PSB and chosen to focus on professionalism as a more measurable and attainable objective. With such an outlook, PSB becomes whatever broadcasters choose to do. Whether the standard is professionalism or the public good, the ever-nagging question is, who defines it? PSB, without a convincing public philosophy of broadcasting, remains open to the charge of self-regarding elitism[4].

So what is PSB? The task can be simplified through understanding that PSB can exist as both a broad classification (ethos) and as a distinct type (structure). In any society, public service broadcasting (lower case) can be required in the attributes of any broadcast system and can also exist as an activity of a particular system known as Public Service Broadcasting (upper case). There is a simple definition which says any programming done in the public interest is public service broadcasting. Who determined public interest? This is quite often the "prickly bush". Each society must develop their own answer to the question. Some answers will work well, others not at all. But the successful working of the answer is an issue of structure, not a determinate of PSB legitimacy.

Included in the historical "root system" of PSB in the UK was the commitment to religious broadcasting. The BBC's first Director-General, John Reith, believed religious (meaning Christian) broadcasting had a central place in programme output. For him religious broadcasting was to provide a "thoroughgoing, manly and optimistic" Christian message. Both the purpose of religious broadcasting and the perception of what constitutes religious broadcasting have changed over time. The postwar years saw a move from Christian to religious broadcasting. One can argue that this was but an outcome of attempts to integrate religious broadcasting into the emerging pluralistic society. By the early 1950s the BBC was more committed to societal expressions of Christian values than making the nation Christian[5].

Many evangelicals feel that there is no longer any place for them in PSB. Therefore, evangelicals show very little concern over the struggle for existence fought by PSB. This is understandable when one begins a discussion on the purpose and function of religious broadcasting within a PSB structure. Different views compete for dominance. All the present positions on the purpose of religious broadcasting can be found in the PSB policies of the BBC over the last fifty years[6]. The pathway travelled by the BBC in religious programming looks very familiar to that travelled by other PSB operations on the European continent and elsewhere in the world.

In 1949 French television regularly broadcast 1 hour 30 minutes of religious programming out of 16 hours output each week; by 1986 only 3 hours Sunday mornings, out of 680 hours weekly of television produced by six channels, were religious in content and inspiration. The percentage of the weekly programme output had fallen from a respectable 10% to a mere 0.5%

The trend indicated by these figures is a common one. Across the world religious programmes have been pushed to the margins of the broadcasting system. In the USA there is little mainline religious programming on the national networks and the electronic church, for all its self-advertisement , has only a small minority, perhaps 7 million viewers, of the US television audience. In Australia and New Zealand the churches are fighting to preserve the place of religion in the public broadcast system. In most of the Third World churches are finding it ever more costly to ensure that even a limited amount of religious material is broadcast on a regular basis.[7]

It is possible to understand why evangelicals are not enamoured of PSB when thinking about religious broadcasting. The track record is not a good one from the evangelical perspective. It is interesting that the reasons given evangelicals most often for denial of PSB access are similar to the charges levelled at PSB by government and commercial broadcasters: low market share, audience pluralism and self-regarding elitism.

No matter how evangelicals are treated when bringing their programmes to PSB, they still have an obligation to PSB. Our faith is not based upon quid pro quo. Public service broadcasting has, as an ideal, respect for the integrity and dignity of the viewer or listener. There is much to commend it to evangelicals for their support.

The public service system, however imperfectly, recognises that religion has a central place in human life, a deregulated commercial system recognises only that religion is a minority interest, like sport, education and even news and public affairs, which can be catered for by specialist channels.[8]

The structures of PSB need continuing examination during this time of rapid technological change. As broadcast distribution channels increase, so too does the danger that PSB will become marginalised. Some argue that public service broadcasting can be satisfied in a deregulated, commercial environment. But "public trust" in the broadcast industry cannot be satisfied through the multiplicity of channels. Public Service Broadcasting is not about offering listeners and viewers more choice; it is about the creative pursuit of broadcasting done in the public interest.

Bill Thatcher is Executive Director of the International Christian Media Commission which has its headquarters in Seattle.

VI

Gabriel Nissim

The French Churches in Public Broadcasting

Christmas 1948. Midnight. An unusual picture appears on France's fifty thousand TV sets. This is the beginning of the world's first televised mass. During his sermon, Cardinal Suhard, Archbishop of Paris, assigned a double target to this new kind of broadcasting; to be a help to all Christians who are confined to their homes, the sick and the old, and to try to reach all people who have moral or religious concerns but who for any reason stay away from church.

Some months later, in October 1949, François Mitterand, who was the member of the government with responsibility for communications, authorised a weekly 90-minute Catholic broadcast on Sunday mornings. *Le Jour du seigneur* was born. It continues today - a weekly 30-minute magazine programme followed by a live broadcast of the mass.

This was a significant decision in a secular state which nonetheless acknowledged the place of the Catholic Church in national life. A few years later, similar decisions were taken in favour of France's other religions. For her part, the Church had made a prophetic move. Father Raymond Pichard and Father Charles Avril (both of them Dominicans) had rightly anticipated the future role of television. They made sure that the efforts of the Church were joined to those of all the other people who were jumping into this new venture.

41

In 1974, when the French state broadcasting corporation ORTF was broken down into several separate organisations, weekly religious broadcasting was officially assigned to TF1 (the state-owned Channel One). The specifications were precise. Nevertheless programme content remained the responsibility of the religious authorities. In 1986, when TF1 was privatised, an amendment was made to the new broadcasting law which attached religious programmes to public service TV. Therefore religious productions were transferred to Antenne 2 which remains a state-owned channel.

Clearly in France it is a duty of public service broadcasting to allow religious TV programmes in an open cultural context and without any economic motive. In accordance with Law No. 86-107, article 56b, of September 30th, 1986: *Every Sunday morning Antenne 2 schedules the religious broadcasts of the main faiths observed in France. These programmes are edited under the direction of the representatives of the religions and consist of the transmission of worship services or religious comments. The production costs are covered by Antenne 2 up to an annually-stipulated maximum figure.*

There is a fairly wide variety in these programmes. Some of them are simply worship-services. Others have an educational target. Current productions for Sunday mornings are:

Muslims	*Connaître l'Islam*	30 mins.
Jews	*A Bible ouverte* and also *Source de vie*	15 to 45 mins.
Orthodox/ Armenian Catholics	*Orthodoxie* alternating with *Chrétiens Orientaux*	up to 30 mins.
Protestants belonging to the Fédération Protestante de France	*Présence Protestante*	30 mins.
Roman Catholics	*Le Jour du seigneur*	90 mins.

The religious programmes start at 8.45 am and end at 12 pm.

In the case of "Le Jour du seigneur", Antenne 2 takes responsibility for two thirds of the production costs. The Catholic *Comité Français de Radio-Télévision* (CFRT) has to find the remainder. As a non-profit organisation, it gets its money from fund-raising efforts and from donations from an average number of 100,000 subscribers. It receives no subsidy from the Catholic hierarchy.

The producers of these programmes are appointed by each religious hierarchy. They are responsible for the substance and form of their programmes; magazine-programmes as well as worship services. They preserve very good relationships with each other (and also with the Antenne 2 representative) and as they all wish to reach a wider public than their own constituency they all favour common productions on a regular basis.

Nevertheless the religious programmes cannot at present escape from the Sunday morning slot and they face tough competition from children's programmes on other channels. The different religious magazines do not attract a market share of more than 5-15% (250,00 to 750,000 viewers). The broadcast of the mass, which is always scheduled at the end of the morning, has about 2,000,000 viewers, which is more or less the normal audience for Antenne 2.

In the future we anticipate an ever-increasing competition between the channels which are already proliferating on cable. We also anticipate increasing financial problems. French Television faces a lack of money. The licence fee is lower in France than in other European countries. Equally on the private channels, the benefits from advertising and channel-charges are low. We may face a difficult fight to keep our programmes alive. As far as the French private (commercial) channels are concerned, we have not yet succeeded in finalizing religious programme projects on a regular basis. This is the tough law of the market.

The lack of religious culture, Christian or otherwise, is increasing and all of us who are concerned about this point to the urgent needs of an up-and-coming generation which seems to show a total ignorance of the religious basis of European culture.

FRENCH TELEVISION CHANNELS

	PUBLIC CHANNELS	PRIVATE CHANNELS	
REGIONAL	FR3	8 MONTBLANC (Alps) TLT TLM TMC Toulouse Lyons Monte Carlo Some main cities	GENERAL INTEREST
NATIONAL	ANTENNE 2 (Channel 2) FR 3 RFO (Overseas Territories)	TF1 (Channel 1) LA CINQ M6	GENERAL INTEREST
NATIONAL	LA SEPT (Cultural French/German)	CANAL PLUS (Films, Sport, News) CANAL J (Children) MCM-EUROMUSIQUE SPORTS 2/3 TV SPORT (Screensport) BRAVO (TV Rebroadcasts) CANAL INFOS (News) CANAL SANTE (Health) CINE CINEMAS - CINE CINEFIL PLANETE (Documentaries)	SPECIAL INTEREST

CHRISTIAN RADIO CHANNELS IN FRANCE

ANGERS	Radio Parabole Anjou
ANNECY	Radio Nessy
AUBENAS	Radio Présence
AUDINCOURT	Radio Omega
AVIGNON	Radio Lumière
BEAUSOLEIL	Radio Evangile
BESANÇON	Radio Horizon
BIARRITZ	Radio Bonne Nouvelle
BOURG-en-BRESSE	Fourvière 01
BREST	Radio Rivages
CASTELMORON/LOT	Radio Espoir
CHAMBERY	Radio Chrétienne Savoie
CLERMONT-FERRAND	Radio Parabole
DIJON	Radio Parabole
FORT DE FRANCE (Martinique)	Radio Saint-Louis
GRENOBLE	R.E.C.I.
LA VERPILLIERE	Radio Colombe
LAVAUR	Radio La Voix du Pech
LE BOUSCAT (Bordeaux)	Radio Harmonie
LE PUY	Radio Source
LYON	Radio Fourvière
MARSEILLE	Radio Dialogue
MONTAUBAN	Radio Espoir 82
MONTIGNY-LES-METZ	Radio Jerico
MONTPELLIER	Association Protestante de Radio TV
	Radio Maguelone
NANCY	Radio Fajet
NANTES	Radio Fidelité
NICE	Radio Accord 06
PARIS	Fréquence Protestante
	Radio Notre-Dame
	Témoignage orthodoxe
POINTRE A PITRE (Guadeloupe)	Radio Massabielle
POITIERS	Radio Accords-Poitou
PONT SAINT ESPRIT	Radio Ecclesia
RENNES	Radio Alpha
ROUEN	Radio Médias
SAINT-DENIS (Ile de la Réunion)	Radio Arc-en-Ciel
SAINT-ETIENNE	RCM Saint-Etienne
SEES	Radio Cathédrale de Sees
STRASBOURG	Radio Arc-en-Ciel
TARBES	Radio "Lourdes Bigorre"
TOULON	Radio Arc-en-Ciel
TOULOUSE	Radio Présence
TOURS	Radio Saint-Martin
VALENCE	Radio Fourvière Valence
VANNES	Radio Sainte-Anne
VILLERS-LES-NANCY	Radio Jerico

Fortunately, we are strengthening our presence in cable television and now in satellite broadcasting. On cable we have some local free broadcasting of religious programmes. Productions are made jointly by the local parishes, the Fédération Protestante de France, the Catholic press and the CFRT. With their local partners, the local churches share the role of editor. CFRT acts as executive producer. As far as satellite is concerned, we are now proceeding with a cultural and educational programme on the Olympus satellite (or a replacement) through the Eurostep programme.

As far as radio is concerned, religious programmes have existed since 1938. They are presently situated on France-Culture (one of the public channels). Every Sunday morning there is a Jewish programme, an Orthodox programme, a Protestant service and a Roman Catholic mass. Some of these broadcasts are also carried by the local stations of Radio France.

Since the deregulation of radio, there are many local religious stations, Jewish, Muslim and Christian (see chart on page 45). These stations are frequently run by volunteers and money comes from donations and from the churches themselves. Their audience can be significant. All the Christian stations belong to the Fédération Française des Radios Chrétiennes. One of them Radio Fourvière of Lyon is an ecumenical station and is heard in several cities thanks to satellite technology.

Religious broadcasting, both on radio and TV, is a strong support to the religions of France for two main reasons:

Firstly, it confirms the faithful in their religious identity amid surroundings that seem all too indifferent to religious matters. The programmes indicate that religion still has its place even within a non-religious society. The programmes demonstrate that religion is not a relic of a past age.

Secondly, the programmes provide an opportunity for the religions to be publicly present in the search for the answers to society's problems. Often the position of the churches is barely, or wrongly, reflected by the media.

Nevertheless, believers have to be careful not to use the audio-visual media merely as a tool in order to get more audience.

They must accept a share (together with TV and radio professionals) in the responsibility for handling this facet of modern culture. And we want not only to deal with modern culture but also with people who are involved as actors in this modern culture. We want to help the media professionals in building a human approach to broadcasting. We must stay close to them in this endeavour understanding that the stakes, the requirements and the risks are very high but that the value is great too.

Gabriel Nissim joined the Dominican Order in 1954. He produced religious programmes at Radio-Douala, Cameroon and later served as Dominican Novice Master of the province of Paris. He is President and artistic producer of the French Sunday programme Le jour du seigneur.

VII

Stephan Abarbanell

The German Churches in Public Broadcasting

Germany's mainline churches, the Protestant Landeskirchen and the Roman Catholic Church, have a privileged place in the German dual broadcasting system. These churches have free airtime for their own programmes on almost every radio and television channel. This applies to the recently-founded private stations as well as to the traditional public broadcasting institutions.

Together with the Jewish community and other "relevant groups" in society, the churches are also members, by law, of the controlling boards of the regional and nationwide broadcasting organisations. The mainline churches also provide both the public and media professionals with a number of different printed publications which try to be as critical and as factual as possible towards all media activities; programming, financing, media politics and ethical questions.

When in 1923 radio started in Berlin, the churches were one of the first groups in society to recognise the advantages of the new wireless. Their request for free airtime was granted in the same year by the local state authorities.

However in 1927 church programming, which by then consisted of live radio sermons and short studio worship services (Morgenfeier), was put under censorship by the government in order to prevent the churches from transmitting "political" statements. In 1939, the Nazis finally closed down all church activities in radio. By then the new medium had become an instrument of propaganda.

After the war the Allies began to see the churches as important groups in society, groups which could help to establish a free and democratic political system in Germany. In November 1948 the churches were allowed to transmit their first worship service in Hamburg. They were also given back their free air time on a number of regional public radio stations. When broadcasting was re-established as a public service in Germany by the victorious Western democracies (the guiding ideal was the concept of the BBC), the churches as well as the Jewish community were asked, on behalf of the whole of society, to become permanent members of the regional public-broadcasting authorities.

Television started in Germany in the early fifties and in 1952 the Lutheran Church of Hamburg and Northwest German Broadcasting tried to transmit a worship service. However, many church leaders had reservations about an attempt to put liturgy onto the small screen. Due to a number of technical difficulties involved in transmitting a worship service in full, it was decided to retain the sermon only and to transfer it to the studio. In May 1954 this studio sermon began what today has become the longest-running programme on German television. It is called *Wort zum Sonntag* (The Word for Sunday) and it is transmitted on Saturday evening. The churches have been able to keep this bi-confessional nationwide programme alive and it sits right in the middle of prime time.

Over the past thirty years, the Protestant Church and Roman Catholic Church have developed an entire infrastructure for their expanding media activities. By the early eighties the churches had approximately 2,000 hours per year on radio and television. This figure however only refers to the public-broadcasting stations of the ARD (regional and nationwide programmes), nationwide ZDF-Television, Deutschlandfunk Radio and Germany's multilingual short-wave world service Deutsche Welle.

GERMAN TELEVISION CHANNELS

	PUBLIC CHANNELS	PRIVATE CHANNELS	
NATIONAL	ARD (Channel 1) — Partnership of the regional broadcasting corporations. Its second outlet is ARD 3 ZDF (Channel 2)	RTL plus SAT 1 Pro 7* Tele 5* (* becoming regional)	GENERAL INTEREST
REGIONAL	SFB Sender Freies Berlin SWF Südwest funk WDR Westdeutscher Rundfunk HR Hessischer Rundfunk BR Bayerischer Rundfunk SDR Süddeutscher Rundfunk NDR Norddeutscher Rundfunk RB Radio Bremen SR Saarländischer Radio MDR in the former DDR	Local affiliates of RTL and SAT 1	
	RIAS-TV, Berlin	K3 TeleWest RNF - live GRF Gruppe Regional Fernsehen	SPECIAL INTEREST
NATIONAL	3 SAT 1 Plus	Sportkanal Premiere Eurosport MTV Super Channel	

Both mainline churches had to invent a new form of minister. They are called Church Commissioners for Radio and Television. Their main task is to find authors, speakers for studio sermons and short viewpoint programmes and local churches for broadcast worship services. They are also supposed to be critical but friendly partners of the broadcasting stations and to be mediators between the media and the churches.

In 1973 the Protestant Landeskirchen and the national Protestant church (EKD) founded the central Joint Protestant Association for Media Communication (GEP) in Frankfurt. It is an umbrella organisation for all kinds of media activities. The director is the spokesperson for media politics on behalf of the central church. The Roman Catholic Church developed almost the same complex structure but set up a smaller secretariat in Bonn.

When commercial broadcasting started in 1984 the German churches did not speak with one voice concerning these new competitors of the public stations. The churches knew on the one hand that they were privileged on the public system. Through the years they had fought for high programme standard. And yet they began to realise that commercial broadcasting could also open up new audiences for the churches, even if the main aim is to make money. After long and complicated discussions, the shape of the churches' involvement in the so-called "new media" is clear. On many regional commercial radio stations the "Landeskirchen" provide informative, documentary and commentary programmes which they produce and finance themselves. They have to provide staff with the capacity to produce programmes in the short and entertaining formats favoured by the private stations.

On two of the four new nationwide satellite television stations, Sat1 and RTLplus, both mainline churches, in a joint initiative signed a contract with the owners which gave the churches up to 45 minutes of free airtime per week. However, due to the vast cost of television the churches only produce about ten minutes of programmes and this is paid for by the two stations. Even though the private stations could make a charge for offering airtime (which according to law they are supposed to do) none of them has so far. One of the reasons for this may be that having the mainline churches as programme partners is a boost to the company image.

From the beginning, the so-called Free Churches (Freikirchen) - the Methodist Church, the Baptist Church, the Union of Free Evangelical Congregations and others - have participated in the privileged role of the Evangelical (Protestant) Church in German broadcasting. And yet they do not themselves have direct access to the system. In almost every area the member churches of the EKD offer some of their own free airtime to these other denominations. In private radio and television, programmes produced by the Free Churches - which have highly-professional standards - are transmitted within the mainline church segments.

The same is true for the evangelicals, a group of firm believers who had already started their radio activities in the fifties. German media laws do not permit them to open up their own stations. But in 1959 the evangelicals founded Evangeliums Rundfunk (ERF) as the German branch of TransWorld Radio and started to transmit their programmes from Monte Carlo on medium and short wave. Today in many church activities and in commercial broadcasting ERF is an accepted professional partner.

In the former GDR, the two big Churches were given access to radio by the Soviet authorities right after the Second World War. They were allowed to transmit sermon-like speeches which of course were censored. In 1978 the state authorities agreed to give the churches access to television on a small but regular basis. Together with the state-run television the churches (mainly the Protestant church) developed programmes which one might call meditative features. But there were heavy restrictions on the choice of topics and the selection of interview guests. Immediately after the breakdown of the Communist regime the churches gained free airtime on almost every regional and nationwide channel. The church was considered to be one of the groups in society who had been in opposition and had finally helped to overthrow the government.

Since October 3rd, 1990 when Germany became one nation again, it has been clear that the broadcasting structure of the former GDR has to be adjusted in accordance with the laws of the Federal Republic. Soon two new big public-broadcasting stations will be founded - in the North and in the South of the former GDR territory. The churches will enjoy the same access to schedules that they have had in the West.

The Landeskirchen in the Eastern parts of Germany as well as the Roman Catholic Church are now developing an infrastructure. Commercial broadcasting is already on the horizon and the churches do not always know how to react at once to all these new possibilities. In fact they lack manpower, knowledge and sufficient money. Some support comes from the member churches of the EKD but in the end they will have to find their own answers to modern media which do not stop at national borders. And what is true for the churches in the East is unfortunately still true for the churches in the West; broadcasting is still not high up on the church's list of priorities.

Stephan Abarbanell is in charge of the German Evangelical Church's department of Radio, Television and Film at GEP (Gemeinshaftswerk der Evangelischen Publizistik) in Frankfurt am Main.

VIII

Brendan Comiskey

Launching Pies or Satellites?

I have been attending media seminars and meetings of various sorts for almost fifteen years now. I am a passionate believer in the need for the Church to use all means possible to preach the Gospel "from the roof tops of the world", to use a papal phrase. I have also invested a great deal of money in communications work in the diocese of which I have been bishop for the past seven years. I preface my remarks on religious broadcasting in this way so that I may not be dismissed as one who knows nothing and cares less about the importance of the media in the life of the Church. When it comes to religious broadcasting I would like to be described as "an optimist without illusion".

Religious broadcasting is far more important in the life of the Church than the great majority of Church leaders realise and a great deal less than some "Church media people" think. The latter make too many assumptions, too many claims based on too little evidence. What is needed in the whole area of religious broadcasting is an injection of interest and capital on the part of Church leaders and an injection of realism and modesty on the part of religious broadcasters and producers. When it comes to discussion of religious broadcasting, there is a danger of having more pies in the sky than satellites!

It is often claimed as a justification of the high costs involved in religious broadcasting that, if St Paul were alive today, he would use television to reach the masses. Would he? American college

Director of Public Relations, Jay Cormier, doubts it very much and makes the point that television "cannot instil a faith that is not there - faith cannot be instilled by simply watching television any more than simply watching Julia Child can make a viewer a gourmet cook. Television can nurture faith and can even make faith grow in a long-fallow field; but television cannot plant the seed. That has to be done within a community of three-dimensional, breathing, loving human beings. In other words, television cannot sow the seeds of faith, but it can water the garden".[9]

When one speaks of "religious broadcasting", a certain definition of "religion" underpins one's remarks. The term "religion" can become so vague as to cover all of life. I like American sociologist Andrew Greeley's definition of religion as "the set of answers a person has available to the fundamental questions of the meaning of life and love, answers which are normally encoded in pictures, images and stories (symbols) and purport uniquely to give purpose and meaning to human existence". Greeley distinguishes religion from doctrine and institution: in the Christian life, religion is "the Jesus story" which provides meaning and purpose to a person's life; religious doctrine and institution are extremely important and necessary as a critique of the story, and a safeguard in its transmission and intellectual explanation.

Religion in Greeley's definition is meaning-giving and man is a meaning-seeking animal; he is also a meaning-making one. Minute by minute he searches for meaning in the situations in which he finds himself. If he is fortunate enough, he finds meaning in what poet Patrick Kavanagh calls[10]

> ...the bits and pieces of Everyday -
> A kiss here and a laugh again, and sometimes tears,
> A pearl necklace round the neck of poverty.

No one is ever completely successful in this search for meaning. Contemplatives are best at staring intently at reality and seeing it as it really is. On the other hand, there are those who settle for "canned meaning", that is, a structure of meaning, an interpretation of reality offered them by others. There is no harm in coming to know another person's life meaning, there is no harm in offering one's own interpretation of reality to others, provided that each person remains his or her own centre of appreciation, criticism and discernment, weighing and evaluating and sifting other interpretations and, hopefully, arriving at one's own unique vision of the real.

Television's reality, unfortunately, too often becomes the only reality for too many people whose "centre of interpretation" is inoperative, who take what is given them as their own reality. The world of soap operas has become the real world for far too many. It is frightening to remember that during the much hyped "Who shot J R?" episode of TV's Dallas, thousands of inquiries from all over the world poured into the real Dallas police station!

When the camera comes in for a close-up, some one once said, sanctifying grace is likely to disappear. God's grace is "such a thing you could not mention without being ashamed of its commonness". Religion's stuff is so close to us we are unable to see it. Many's the time one is teased for not being able to see something which is "right under your nose", which is "staring you straight in the face". Some Christians are so scandalised by the Incarnation that they can never believe that the kingdom of God is closer to a person than is his or her own very self; it is within us. When something is "right under one's nose", or "staring one straight in the face", it is often difficult to see. For example, it is impossible to read a newspaper or view a painting which is too close. One needs to put it away from oneself a slight distance to get it into perspective.

It is difficult to capture in one's own life - people spend lifetimes of prayer in the task - this stuff of religion, not to mention communicating it to others. Prayer and silence and periods of retreat and reflection are necessary in the Christian life precisely for this purpose. The problem of religious broadcasting is the challenge of preaching writ large, and the problem of preaching is already written large enough! According to St Paul's First Letter to the Corinthians, only the person who has the mind of Christ can teach the hidden wisdom of God - "the things that no eye has seen and no ear has heard, things beyond the mind of man" - because this has been revealed to him through the

Spirit. It should not be too readily assumed that religious broadcasters have appropriated the mind of Christ. His name is seldom enough invoked at international gatherings of Christian broadcasters. There is likely to be more talk about satellites than Saviour.

When one is "ashamed of its commonness", embarrassed by its Incarnation or unable to see God's presence in history because it is right under one's nose, or staring one right in the face, it is necessary to create an artificial salvation fiction of one's own. Our inability to see that the "world is charged with the grandeur of God" makes it necessary to construct a world of our own which, to use Hopkins' description, "wears man's smudge and shares man's smell". We end up cultivating a plot of spiritual ground in the suburbs of reality. We invent creatures from outer space. Take the legendary E.T. for example; much has been written supporting the claim that this film "reinvents the Incarnation". Isn't it extraordinary that in an age which has declared God to be dead, mankind has now proceeded to populate the world with all kinds of mythical extra-terrestrial creatures? One priest-columnist recently expressed the opinion that "Jesus was put to death because he sacked the skies of mystery and resolutely claimed its presence in what we would prefer not to deal with, namely, our lives, and the groan and promise that are the present moment".

Religious broadcasting must come to terms with "what we would prefer not to deal with" if it is to overcome the temptation to create its own (unreal) world. A remark made by a Harvard professor, Harvey Cox, in the 1960s has greatly influenced my approach to religion and the media. Up until that time, many of the American "secular" newspapers contained Religious Supplements which gave fairly extensive coverage to Church events and personnel. When one paper after another discontinued these supplements, there was no scarcity of laments from prominent Church people. Professor Cox did not share this view and remarked at the time that God had escaped from the "churchy" inside pages to the wider reaches of the front pages where the real world of real people was being reported.

Professor Cox was echoing the sentiments of the Second Vatican Council's Pastoral Constitution on the Church in the

Modern World: "The joys and the hopes, the griefs and the anxieties of the men of this age, especially those who are poor or in any way afflicted, these too are the joys and hopes, the griefs and anxieties of the followers of Christ. Indeed, nothing genuinely human fails to raise an echo in their hearts." Such joys and hopes, but more particularly the griefs and anxieties of people today, especially the poor and the afflicted, are much more likely to appear on front pages than in "Church news" columns. Religious broadcasting, if is to be authentic, must connect with the real world of God's people, it must celebrate it, inspire it and be inspired by it; finally it must report on it.

Firstly, authentic religious broadcasting must make connections with the very real and very ordinary life of people. When it is not thus connected, it slips its moorings and becomes what Rev Miles O'Brien Riley, a veteran of Christian broadcasting, calls "cotton candy religion, with Jesus on a smile button, religion that is a big warm blanket that you can wrap yourself up in when you're sad". William F. Fore, United Methodist minister and Secretary for Communications for the US National Council of Churches is also extremely critical of television evangelists "for providing trivial and superficial religion, a quick fix to people's anxiety". The fictitious minister who practises this kind of media ministry in my own country is called "Father Trendy" and is the subject of much lampooning and cartooning. He is unreal.

Religious broadcasting is not connected with the real world when it pretends to be something it is not. One terrifying example of this is the so-called "Electronic Church" in America. First and foremost, this was never a church. A church is a community of people, bound together in faith, supporting one another in good times and in bad. An audience, on the other hand, according to Cox, "is not a congregation. An audience is a mass of people who don't know each other, who can't really meet to be together, to support each other ....I think it would be much better if the people who have been attracted to [televangelists] would somehow return to [their local] church where there is a continuation of fellowship with other people...where there's ongoing life and prayer and gathering in spirit." Religious broadcasting must connect its listener and viewer with community.

Secondly, authentic religious broadcasting must celebrate God's presence in the midst of his people. Worship programmes do this and make a valuable contribution especially to the lives of those who cannot or do not attend church. Neither is it an entirely valid exercise to criticise these as "preaching to the converted". The converted need all the preaching they can get! Especially those who think they are "converted". In any case, "conversion" is a lifelong process, not the end of faith's journey.

Thirdly, religious broadcasting should inspire and be inspired by God's people. Inspirational reflections such as those provided at the beginning of the day by BBC Radio 4 are genuinely helpful in helping one raise one's thoughts and hearts to God. All of us need help, especially where technological knowledge has ousted wisdom. Or, put in the more poetic lines of poet Patrick Kavanagh,

> We have tested and tasted too much, lover -
> Through a chink too wide there comes in no wonder.
> But here in the Advent-darkened room
> Where the dry-black bread and the sugarless tea
> Of penance will charm back the luxury
> Of a child's soul, we'll return to Doom
> The knowledge we stole but could not use.

The worldwide appeal of the recently-deceased Graham Greene is proof that the greatest inspiration often comes from telling stories of God's power and grace in the lives of others. It is also another way of anchoring a religious broadcaster in the real world. There is no need for the kind of gimmickry which has characterised the Electronic Church in America and certainly not for the artificial world where, in the words of Lutheran theologian and ecumenist Martin Marty, "there is no cross. In a half-hour, they have to convert you (which trivialises what conversion means), heal you (which is hokey), promise success (people on the shows have overcome alcoholism, are Miss America, or play in the National Football League) and entertain (so they find even more expensive sets with more fountains and glamour which detract from the world of the suffering) .... Christianity and celebrity do not go together. A celebrity has a big ego and needs to feed it. The shows misportray government, humanism, and mainline religions. They don't convert; they confirm". Sometimes the constraints of broadcasting are of such a type as to make it impossible to communicate the Christian message. It would be better not to broadcast than to do it at too high a price and I mean the price of integrity.

Fourthly, religious broadcasting can instruct. The best use of television for the purpose of instruction were the famous TV programmes during the 1950s of Bishop Fulton Sheen who, with a blackboard and chalk and the assistance of an off-camera aide (his "angel") who cleaned the board, enthralled America and won top TV ratings during the 1950s in the USA. Of that man it could probably be said that we shall not see the likes of him again. Neither shall we see the type of medium which allowed him access. Fulton Sheen was entertaining and instructive, but he was never mere entertainment. Religion should bring joy. Preaching, for example, should be, in part at least, entertaining. But when the constraints of television call for mere entertainment, then one should resist the temptation to betray the Christian message by portraying it as such. Mankind's salvation does not exclude joy but it is not entertainment!

"Communicate or die!" the Church is often warned. Communicate, not entertain! I suggest that entertainment is the medium through which clowns, comics and comedians communicate: entertain or die. It is interesting that comedians, for example, when they have a bad night on stage, speak of "dying" on stage. When a Church person tries to become a mere entertainer, it grossly distorts the Christian message. Such a person succeeds in communicating - entertaining, rather - and dying at one and the same time!

Fifthly and finally, religious broadcasting can inform. Again, however - and this applies more to television than it does to radio - if the message communicated is forced to conform to an entertainment model, the result is not so much a bias against the message as a bias against understanding. A programme may be presented as a forum for discussion, but its primary if not sole purpose is to entertain the viewer with the sight of verbal gladiators trying to overcome one another by fair means and foul.

Salman Rushdie's description of literature is equally applicable to some discussion programmes on television: "the one place where, ... we hear voices talking about everything in every possible way". At the end of such a programme, people are more confused and less informed that they were at the beginning. But, it may be argued, no one will stay tuned to a dull show. No, they won't. But need all other forms of human interchange and communication except entertainment be dull?

I have been in "the media wars" for more than fifteen years now - television, radio and the print media - but I would question the assumption that, when a bishop, for example, refuses an invitation to appear on a programme, this represents a lost opportunity. Must every request be taken as a splendid chance to communicate the message "from the roof tops of the world". What naivete! Is no one willing to admit that church people are often "set up" and merely used as props to communicate the programme maker's message? Must Church leaders become performing bears for the media circus? Some programmes provide opportunities; others don't. One needs to distinguish.

It is not cynical to say that the media often come to a Church press conference with a story already written. They come looking for "an angle". The coverage often bears no resemblance whatsoever to what was the main purpose for which the conference was called in the first instance. It will be argued, unfairly I believe, that if the people responsible were skilled enough and if more resources were made available - always more resources - this could be avoided. The truth is that it can't. It takes little enough brains and less talent to "put a spin" on any story.

Remember the lesson of the newly-appointed cardinal arriving in Rome for his very first visit to the Eternal City. A member of the international press corps present at a press conference inquired what the cardinal intended to do in his leisure hours in Rome. "Will you be going to any night clubs?" queried a reporter from the cardinal's own home country. Taken aback and never having associated the centre of Christendom with night clubs, the somewhat startled cardinal asked, "Are there night clubs in Rome?" No prize for guessing the next day's

headlines. WHERE ARE NIGHTCLUBS? NEW CARDINAL'S FIRST IN-
QUIRY UPON ARRIVAL IN ROME.

We would all be well advised to become more aware of the
"constraints of the media". And please don't tell me that I'm
not sufficiently optimistic. An optimist with illusions is a fool.

*Brendan Comiskey is Bishop of Ferns in southeast Ireland and has
been President of the Catholic Communications Institute of Ireland
and Chairman of the Episcopal Commission for Communication
since 1982.*

IX

Anthony Pragnell

Opportunity and Limitation

The changes which are taking place in European broadcasting
largely stem from technological development, not simply because that enables more services to be transmitted more effi-
ciently but also because an increase in the number of services
which can be broadcast has led to a change in attitudes towards
regulation. What seemed reasonable in days when access to the
air was regarded as a privilege to be exercised by a few carefully-
selected organisations is no longer considered appropriate at a
time when access is more widely available.

Changing Technology

Technological changes are of two kinds: those which improve
the technical quality of what we see and hear; and those which
increase the range of services available. Examples of the first
kind of change would include the introduction of higher definition into television; the conversion of television from mono-
chrome to colour; the introduction of FM radio (which also
opened up the possibility of increasing the number of radio
stations); and the coming of stereo sound.

The most dramatic example of the second kind of change is the
introduction of satellite broadcasting (which covers both television and sound broadcasting). Additionally, however, the
development of cable systems has provided the public with an

increased choice of programmes. In sound, too, it is possible (though not certain enough to be relevant to current plans for religious broadcasting) that by the end of the century digital audio broadcasting will have progressively opened up new possibilities.

Paying for Improvements in Quality

Improvements in the quality of transmission and reception of existing services are always likely to be costly. But their introduction is to some extent an option both for the programme providers and for the public. The providers will make qualitative improvements only if they can afford to do so, and those which are self-supporting will always consider how cost-effective such improvements will be (as Sky Television no doubt did when deciding to use the PAL system on the SES Astra satellite rather than going for the MAC system which would give more potential for further technical development). The public too are free to decide whether to equip themselves to receive the improved quality of transmissions; if they do not do so, they may be depriving themselves of some increased enjoyment, but the range of programmes available is not diminished.

Paying for Expansion of Services

Technological developments leading to an increase in the number of programmes will also be costly. In some cases, where they represent an expansion of existing systems (for example, BBC 2 and Channel Four in the United Kingdom), development money can be found from within those systems. Where, however, they are entirely new, sufficient money must be in place from the start when the eventual audience has to be wooed away from other established and popular channels and has, in some cases, to be persuaded to pay for the domestic equipment needed to receive the new offerings.

All this is to say that, while technological ingenuity can do many things in broadcasting, it can only do so if there is enough money available to finance it. It also emphasises the need for religious-broadcasting plans to be soundly based. We must constantly bear in mind the character in *The Loved One* who had to learn a trade because her father had lost his money in religion.

A Continuum of Change

Although the present decade will see dramatic developments in Europe's broadcasting, we should not forget the equally important changes which have taken place through a process of evolution since the Second War. In that period, for instance, advertising has become accepted as a proper means of financing television and radio services, although normally as part of a mixed economy and with licence fees as the other main source of income.

We have also come, though perhaps less readily, to accept, or tolerate, the growing place of market economics in broadcasting. Until relatively recently, the authorities, governmental or otherwise, which decided which bodies should be allowed to broadcast, were anxious to be sure that those so allowed had enough money, initially and in reserve, to survive even if the economic climate turned against them. Now, the authorities are more likely in the case of the new services to let entrepreneurs make their own appraisal of the risks they are running and to see them take the consequences if things go wrong. This is one of the results of the increase of pluralism in broadcasting.

Pluralism in Broadcasting

INCREASE IN THE NUMBER OF SERVICES

Even before the coming of satellite broadcasting, there was a large increase in the number of services that were becoming available. In terrestrial television, the number of domestic channels almost doubled in Western Europe, from 36 to 68 in the 1980-90 decade. In radio, the number of regional and local stations has grown quickly to over 4,000, with national services totalling around 100.

BREAKING DOWN OF MONOPOLIES

However, pluralism is not to be measured in numbers of services only. There has also been a progressive erosion of the original monopolies or oligopolies which used to form the original structures of Europe's broadcasting.

Thus, in France we have seen in television the privatization of TF1 and the emergence of two new private channels (La Cinq and M6) and one pay-television channel (Canal Plus), all operating alongside the public service channels (Antenne 2 and FR3). In radio, France has nine major commercial networks and some 1,000 commercial local radios.

Belgium, to take another example, traditionally cherished its linguistic duopoly of RTBF (French) and BRT (Flemish). In the late 1980s, however, two commercially-operated television channels were introduced: TVi for the French community and VTM for the Flemish one. In radio, there are national networks for the linguistic communities and also 400 independent local commercial stations in Flanders and 300 in the French-speaking areas.

In the Netherlands we have the "pillarised" system of NOS and the eight broadcasting associations (four of which have a religious base: KRO Catholic, NCRV liberal Protestant, EO evangelical Protestant and VPRO originally of a progressive Protestant background, although now largely secularised in its output). This system already has to operate alongside several hundred local broadcasting stations (radio and television) and, in television, has to compete with foreign services, and in particular the highly popular and mainly Dutch-language RTL4, which are distributed by cable to about three-quarters of the population. The Dutch government is reviewing the whole structure of broadcasting and it may well be that in the near future there will be further competition from nationally-based commercial television stations.

As a final example, we can take Italy, where the monopoly of RAI, the public service system, was among the first to be broken in Europe, the breach being probably the most comprehensive so far. The process got under way in the early 1970s when commercial interests were able to exploit loopholes in the Broadcasting Law to erode RAI's radio and television monopoly at the local level. These interests then moved on to link many of the local stations into national and interregional networks. In radio there are now some 4,500 private FM stations. In television, the most powerful private company (Fininvest, owned by the redoubtable Silvio Berlusconi) owns three national networks which compete strongly with RAI's three services. In recent years, RAI has fallen behind in its struggle to retain half the Italian audience.

DIVERSITY OF PROGRAMME SOURCE

Despite the inroads which are being made into the primacy of the large, established broadcasting systems, they remain of major importance. For the last twenty years or more, there has been in the United Kingdom and elsewhere criticism from creative people engaged (or wanting to be engaged) in television production. The criticism has been directed against the great power which resides within the organisations in choosing who can provide the material which is broadcast.

It was the force of this argument for opening up broadcasting to include those who are not permanently associated with the broadcasting organisations which, in 1977, led the United Kingdom Annan Committee to recommend the establishment of an Open Broadcasting Authority. This idea, though not accepted, led to the introduction of Channel Four in the early 1980s. Channel Four was, and remains, mandated to give emphasis in its programme schedules to productions from independent companies. (In 1989/90, 54% of the Channel's total hours of commissioned programmes came from independent producers. They were responsible for 71% of commissioned programme costs and 58% of total programme costs.)

More recently, it has become Government policy (being implemented by the broadcasters) that ITV and BBC should obtain at least 25% of their original production from independent companies. A similar requirement, although at the much lower level of 10%, has been incorporated into the European Commission's 1989 Directive on Transfrontier Television.

THE EFFECTS OF COMPETITION

Lord Reith once asked CBS executives (at a time when CBS claimed to be the quality leader among the US networks) how they could successfully and simultaneously serve both God and Mammon.

The ability of existing European broadcasters to continue to perform that dual service is now being put under pressure. First of all, there is the loss of audience to new channels. Thus, in Western Germany where traditionally in television the two public systems, ARD and ZDF, had a virtual monopoly of the national audience, in cabled homes (which currently represent about 25% of the total and which are growing in number), the five largest shares of viewing in 1990 were

ARD 1	21.5%
ZDF	19.9%
RTL plus	16.2%
Sat 1	14.9%
ARD III	7.5%

In Italy, too, as has already been mentioned, RAI currently seems to be falling behind the commercial television channels in share of audience, probably obtaining less than 45%.

These falls in the audience are, of course, directly reflected in the revenue-earning capacity of services wholly or partly dependent on advertising. They are indirectly reflected in those services which are financed from licence fees. Here, falling audiences may well cause governments to hesitate to maintain fees at past levels. Often, too, they may demand (not always wrongly) that the broadcasting services tighten their belts. There will also be pressures, when there is a growing number of services providing material which is predominantly entertaining, for the licence fee systems to concentrate more on the educative and informative. The services will also be told, as has the BBC, to look for alternative sources of income by maximising the incidental value of their output - through more effective selling abroad, by merchandising activities, and so on.

Regulation, Deregulation and Reregulation

It will be clear so far how much deregulation has taken place, above all in freer access to the air as the available frequency space has been expanded. In radio this has happened most notably through the use of FM, in terrestrial television by more efficient use of the spectrum, as well as by cabling, and by the use of satellites.

The increase in the number of services has also had a compounding effect on deregulation: the more services there are, the less may it be necessary to apply to *all* of them exactly the same set of rules as was considered appropriate for a far smaller number of national cornerstone services.

In a number of countries there has also been a reappraisal of the scope and procedures of regulatory bodies. In the United Kingdom, for example, there has been, with the introduction of the Independent Television Commission and the Radio Authority (both successors to the Independent Broadcasting Authority), the intention that the new bodies should operate with a lighter touch. They are also to exercise their powers of control retrospectively, adjudicating and correcting (including the power to levy hefty fines) after the event.

But this seemingly lighter and less restrictive regime has entailed a fair amount of regulation of a different kind and the more specific codification of past practices. Thus, an applicant for a new licence for Channel 3 in the UK beginning in 1993 would receive at least fifteen documents from the Independent Television Commission including seven codes or guidance notes on programmes, advertising, sponsorship and technical matters.

It should also be added finally that, despite all procedural changes, most of the important public service elements which have always informed the ITV (now Channel 3) and Channel Four programmes will be maintained in the future.

In France, TF1, even though privatised, remains one of the three original national television channels, each with a distinctive remit, under the surveillance of the *Conseil Supérieur de l'Audiovisuel* which covers also the newer services.

These and other cases confirm the durability of existing regulative principles and practices, even though they may not operate in their full rigour on the new services.

Trends for the Future

As part of the continuum of change, the following main trends can be identified:

THE GROWING INTERNATIONALISATION OF BROADCASTING

As well as the well-established international audiences in the cable-friendly countries (90% of television homes in Belgium; approaching 80% in the Netherlands; and 70% in Luxembourg and Switzerland) television satellite broadcasting will continue to show dramatic growth in number of channels available. (Between 1989 and 1991 the numbers of satellites operating and of channels available will effectively double from 9 to 17 and from 67 to 138 respectively).

THE DEMAND FOR PROGRAMME MATERIAL TO FEED NEW SERVICES

In 1980, television programme hours in Europe totalled about 120,000 a year; the figure has now risen to some 300,000 and by the mid-1990s is expected to exceed one million.

THE QUEST FOR INCREASED REVENUE

An increase in the number of services and in hours of transmission does not imply an automatic proportionate growth in revenue: governments are reluctant to increase licence fees and advertising tends to follow audience levels and not the number of advertising outlets. We can observe the following steps being taken to expand revenue:

> relaxation of some of the existing rules about the amount of advertising which can be shown;

> the growing toleration of sponsorship, long regarded as an undesirable prejudicing of broadcasters' freedom in making up their schedules;

> the introduction of subscription and other pay-television services.

Christian Communication in a Changing World

There will, of course, continue to be in Europe a wide diversity of practice about religious broadcasting. The Netherlands, with its four religious broadcasting associations, will seem to many Christian communicators to be their Shangri-la. In Portugal the Catholic Church owns a major radio station and would like to play a prominent part in television. The diversity will continue and is not likely to be quickly affected by wider changes in the broadcasting landscape. But, it is still worth trying to identify some possible general lines of advance and some issues which need to be tackled in the coming decade.

The Scope of New Religious Services

We should perhaps begin by assuming, if for no other reason than that frequency space has already been used up, that it is fruitless to consider establishing new major terrestrial radio or television services. In practice, for new radio services, there will be scope in local FM stations. In television, the most obvious place for new religious broadcasting is to be found in satellite broadcasting.

In radio, new services will be operating in a highly competitive environment. A recent study, *Radio 2000*, prepared for the European Broadcasting Union by the European Institute for the Media, confirmed that the trend in Europe is "towards dedicated channels.... designed to offer a clearly identified programme service to a targeted and defined audience". Before a religious channel could be set up anywhere, there would need to be a rigorous preliminary study to see if it could rely on getting a niche audience large enough to support it (if it had to earn its own living from advertising) or to justify a sufficiently large subvention from church sources to keep it going.

The use of television satellite broadcasting would initially raise the issue of cost. One estimate of the amount needed for an ecumenical European channel transmitting for ten hours a day is at least £100m, which certainly does not seem on the high side.

Satellite broadcasting makes possible an international audience and it seems unrealistic to think that the programming of a satellite service would not take account of this. In principle, a number of different religious channels could broadcast: there is no "built-in electronic ecumenism" (to use a phrase of Colin Morris). However, cost may well be a deciding factor in favour of the inter-church approach.

Religious Broadcasting in other Services

Whatever may be the position over dedicated Christian services, it will remain important that religious broadcasting should not be displaced from other services. Competition may make the self-supporting services more reluctant to include material which may have only specialist audience appeal; on the other hand, if they are

71

short of programme material, they might be receptive to offerings from the churches. However, unless such offerings come from a wide variety of sources, problems of balance between different approaches and traditions could arise.

In the case of the public service broadcasters, competition should have less effect on their willingness to provide religious programmes. But it may not be wholly without effect and it will be important that religious interests should continue to press the case convincingly for religious programmes being regarded as an essential ingredient in a high-quality and wide-ranging programme service.

PAYING FOR RELIGION

We know that in France religious organisations have to pay towards the cost of their programmes on television (the annual Catholic broadcasting budget is some £2m). In the United Kingdom, as elsewhere, the idea of the religious bodies having to pay for broadcasting time has not arisen until now. But religious advertising and sponsorship will, subject to strict conditions, be allowed on the advertising-supported services. It is not necessary to discuss here whether this departure from past policy is a good or a bad thing, but it is an indication that, in future, and not only in the United Kingdom, there will be wider opportunities available for religious interests to pay for entry to the air.

Broadcasting companies short of funds in a competitive environment may also be willing to accept ready-made programmes from religious groups without having to meet the full cost of such programmes. These possibilities raise opportunities, and equally obvious problems of balance and quality in programming.

Anthony Pragnell was Deputy Director-General of the Independent Broadcasting Authority, London, until 1983.

X

Bob Towler

Changing the Ecology of Broadcasting

The assumption that the new era of broadcasting which we are now entering is simply one which presents new opportunities is an incomplete assumption. That there will be new opportunities is undoubtedly true, but the new era means much more than that: broadcasting is about to become a whole new ballgame. Our thinking about it will have to change much more radically than most people have grasped so far.

In the Autumn of 1982 the United Kingdom had a new, fourth, television channel. (Actually it had two new channels, but S4C in Wales is a special case). Channel 4 did indeed provide new opportunities without changing the whole ecology of broadcasting. It did so because it was to be a channel which commissioned and bought programmes but did not make them. The programmes broadcast were to be made by producers who would be acting independently, not within a hierarchy such as the BBC or Thames Television. The ideas for programmes, the organisation of production, the style and techniques employed were all to be wide-open. On this channel there would be no house style such as that which marked, say, documentaries from London Weekend Television or arts programmes on BBC. Here was a chance for new voices to be heard. The chance was taken. New production companies sprang up like mushrooms until now, nearly ten years later, there is a flourishing independent production sector like nowhere else in the world.

There were new opportunities for religious programmes as for all other categories of programmes. So how did the churches respond? Without reference to either Channel 4 or to the regulating authority, the IBA, they established the British Churches Committee for Channel 4. Given a modest sum of money, including a grant from Channel 4 itself, the committee set out to find good ideas and talented film makers whom they could back with their money. The intention was to assist the development of proposals which could then, with luck, be funded through to production by Channel 4. Well-intentioned though it was, the experiment was a total failure.

There were two principal reasons: First, a committee which meets two or three times a year is wholly unsuited to finding and promoting programme ideas. Far more effective for this task was a full-time commissioning editor, responsible for religious programmes. (In the first years of the Channel's life John Ranelagh was Commissioning Editor.) Secondly, a committee with only £10,000 to spend is unlikely to have much influence. A commissioning editor on the other hand, seeing the germ of a good idea, can afford £5,000 to pay for it to be developed. He can also be in touch with suitable writers, researchers, presenters, producers and directors. The churches made a brave try but it was doomed from the start. Nor can one see any other ways in which they might have helped new religious voices to reach the screen, at least not without making serious money available.

The birth of Channel 4 genuinely represented a range of new opportunities for religious broadcasting, and it deserves to be noted that the churches have found no way of responding to those opportunities. My point, however, is a different one. One new channel, in addition to the existing three (especially since it was based on the principle of commissioning programmes from the independent producers) is one scenario in which it is sensible to talk of *opportunities*. However the scene which confronts us now is of a different order.

As cable takes off, we are seeing a transition from four channels to fifty-plus channels. As the report of the committee chaired by

Alan Peacock noted, airtime ceases to be a precious resource under the new scenario and television loses much of its uniqueness as a medium, becoming much more like the publishing of books, of magazines or of newspapers. Proliferation means that there can be a specialist channel alongside those which are popular. Commercial viability is the only check.

WHERE WILL NEW RELIGIOUS PROGRAMMES COME FROM?

A word must be said about what constitutes religious broadcasting. Questions of definition are always tedious and can often amount to no more than the splitting of hairs but to ignore them completely can be dangerous. To assume that we all know what we mean by religious broadcasting, and that we all mean the same thing, can result in time-wasting confusion.

In truth, no substantive definition of religious broadcasting can be found any more than we can find one for religion itself. A religious programme is one made by the religious department of broadcasting company or paid for from a budget labelled "religion". In other words religious programmes can be identified by their *source*, rather than by their *content*. This observation is useful because it then prompts us to ask what are the sources of religious programmes. There are three sources:

First, there are the religious departments and budgets of the regulated broadcast networks. (The unregulated networks make or commission virtually no religious programmes).

Second, there are the religious institutions themselves, be they Christian churches or the institutions of non-Christian religions. This source contributes very little indeed to the broadcast output worldwide though it is conceivable that churches or their specialist agencies could make and pay for programmes which could be offered to broadcasters. However, there is no sign at present that the policies and priorities of the churches are about to change in such a way as to alter this situation.

Third, there are the communications-led religious groups which exist principally for the purpose of making and distributing programmes to promote a particular religious message.

I make this three-fold distinction only to point out that any new religious programmes to fill the airtime of proliferating channels are likely to come from groups dedicated to the propagation of very specific messages.

Do Religious Programmes Travel Well?

An opportunity in religious broadcasting that I want to single out is distribution. In recent years there have been attempts especially by European broadcasters to share programmes. For example the religious broadcast organisations of five countries might agree to contribute one programme to a series which all of them will then share. Such schemes are not exclusive to the religious output.

The outcome of such experiments is rarely successful since cultural differences are greater than they first appear. International co-productions face problems when one particular partner does not have effective editorial control. On the other hand there are many programmes, made with specific national audiences in mind, which travel well.

Three films which I have bought for transmission on Channel 4, each a German-language programme, well illustrate the point. *The Space In The Heart Of The Lotus* was made for Bavarian Television and ORF in Austria by an independent. It was a 60-minute profile of Dom Bede Griffiths, the very English Benedictine monk, who lives in a Hindu-style Ashram in India seeking to draw on the spiritual traditions of the East in ways which complement and enrich the Western traditions. It was even more accessible to a British audience since Bede Griffiths, speaking to camera in English, did not require the subtitles needed for a German audience and the commentary was easily re-voiced into English.

Almost Christmas was a virtually-mute drama. The story was told by action and image, with music and prose commentary on the sound track. A similar film called *Funeral Sermons* was made with almost no sync sound and therefore could be re-voiced with equal ease. Of Channel 4 programmes which have sold well abroad, three typical examples are *Milingo*, telling the story of Archbishop Milingo; *Testament*, the 7-part series of the history of the Bible narrated by John Romer and *Shadow On The Cross*, a film about Christian anti-semitism.

Not all programmes will travel, of course, especially if they deal with very specific domestic issues or are concerned with matters that are too current. Many others, perhaps 40% of Channel 4's religious output, will travel - particularly if the programmes are made with the possibility of re-versioning in mind. Too many pieces-to-camera create a problem but often the same point can be made in a different way or the person concerned can be filmed doing something else while the interview material is carried in voice-over. And, of course, re-versioning can be done well or badly, clumsily or with delicacy. There is a wealth of programming available. And yet there is no specialist distributor of religious programming who travels the world buying and selling. A distribution house specialising in religious programmes would succeed if it met four criteria:

First, the right people would be needed, people with both good programme-judgement and with the ability to sell, people moreover with the time to build relationships with the makers and the buyers of religious programmes in many territories.

Secondly, the list would need to contain non-religious as well as religious programmes since - we must face the fact - religion is not an inspiration for most of those people responsible for buying-in programmes. Buyers from other countries may acquire a British film because it is a good film and include it in their general output not even knowing that in Britain it was a "religious programme". An attractive list requires variety as well as speciality.

Thirdly, such an operation would need to be run on commercial lines, employing commercial judgements.

Fourthly, a good distributor would invest in some programmes in order to buy the involvement which might ensure that saleable programmes were made. One such distributor house exists, in embryo, in Britain in the sales department of CTVC in Bushey.

Dr. Bob Towler is Commissioning Editor, Religion, at Channel 4, London.

XI

Eric Shegog

A Blueprint for Britain

The Broadcasting Act 1990, together with recent technological developments, offers Christians in Britain new and exciting prospects. The question we have to face is how we should respond to these new opportunities. The way we respond will be largely determined by four factors:

First: The framework laid down by the new regulatory bodies, the Independent Television Commission (ITC), and the Radio Authority (RA). The requirements laid down by the programme codes of these two bodies are different, therefore our responses will have to be different. It will be a question of horses for courses!

Second: The Churches will have to decide at what *level* of broadcasting they should respond. Should we have a local target? If so, should this be local radio or community radio or a local cable network? Or, should we be thinking at the national level, with programming for a network cable channel or the main channels which are now required to devote 25% of their output (except news and current affairs) to independent producers?

Third: How far should any particular denomination go it alone, and, given the different doctrinal or theological positions, how far is an ecumenical approach possible, or even desirable?

Fourth, and probably most significant: How much will it cost?

Before I answer these questions with reference to the British scene, I think there is a more fundamental question which needs to be addressed, and which is frequently overlooked by Christians. Why should Christians bother to be involved with mass means of communication at all? After all they have more than enough to be getting on with, maintaining churches and schools, and an extensive Church infrastructure. There is one school of thought represented by Neil Postman, Professor of Communications at New York University, which believes we should not get involved with television. He argues that it is the nature of television to trivialise everything. Television is best suited to answering *wants* rather than meeting *needs*. However, Jesus was not in the business of offering people what they wanted, but what they needed. By playing to television's strengths, with its emphasis on personalities, entertainment and over-simplification, so that complex issues have to be explained in short soundbites, the Gospel runs the risk of being trivialised into what Kierkegaard called twaddle. So the argument runs.

For other Christians, television is not to be touched or trifled with, because it is utterly secular. Following the writer of John's Gospel who prayed that Christians should be kept from the world, Christ is seen in the American theologian Reinhold Niebuhr's terms as being "over against" Culture. Some would even go as far as Tillich, the German theologian. He would have described television as demonic, had he lived long enough.

Television is demonic, so Tillich would argue, because it takes what is not God - money, status or power - and pretends that it is. It tempts viewers to give in to the demons of sensuality. So, in St Paul's words, "That which I would not do, I do".

This is clearly an extreme position. Some Christians resolve the dilemma by arguing that the end justifies the means. If the Kingdom can be extended by using this tool of the devil, then we are justified in using it. As General Booth said, "Why should the devil have all the best tunes?"

Personally I see no reason why churches should not be involved with broadcasting. They have the Lord's mandate to carry the

Good News throughout the world. Jesus used contemporary methods to communicate His message. He used the techniques of the rabbis, for example, and open-air preaching. St Paul went into the market place in Athens to communicate with passers-by, not very successfully as it happens. The monks of the Middle Ages used illustrations in their manuscripts and when Gutenberg invented movable type the Church moved into publishing in a big way.

It seems perfectly proper therefore that we should use modern equivalents, provided that we recognise that any means of communication influences the way we communicate so that the message has to be tailored to the medium. As Albert van den Heuvel has wisely said on numerous occasions, the Churches must decide whether they wish to *use* the medium of radio and television or to *serve* it. This means that we do have to recognise broadcasting's strengths and weaknesses. It is not an appropriate medium for lecturing people, or for trying to deal with complicated arguments. But it is, for example, a marvellous medium for telling stories.

We also need to remind ourselves that religious broadcasting is not a substitute for the work of the local church. We are not in the business of creating a community of faith that exists solely on the airwaves, and which makes no more demands on the viewer than to sit in front of the television screen or radio. Any religious programming must be seen as part of the wider mission of the Churches and complementary to it. At the end of the day any broadcasting we do is pre-evangelism, pointing people to communities of faith, where the real evangelism begins. Having established that we should, as Christians, use the electronic media, how then should churches, congregations, and individual Christians respond?

So - what are the opportunities available to us, and how far is our response determined by the regulators? In Britain these are the Independent Television Commission (ITC) and the Radio Authority. The BBC is both regulator and broadcaster.

First, there is the public service broadcasting system: BBC television channels 1 and 2, the commercially-funded TV channels 3, 4 and (when it is available) 5, BBC Radio's five channels, and BBC local radio. Where the BBC is concerned, religious broadcasting on both television and radio is in the hands of a specialist department, many of whose staff are Christians. Some of the larger Channel 3 companies also have specialist departments.

As far as audience-levels are concerned, it is fairly certain that the established television channels will continue to attract major audiences and, in the case of the commercially-funded channels, the advertising revenue as well. This means that in an increasingly competitive environment programmes should be well resourced. Religious programmes should therefore share proportionally in these major audiences, depending on how well they are made, how imaginative they are, and whether they are scheduled at a time when significant audiences are available. Even if the programmes do not attract large audiences, they are at least assured of their place - because profit is not the only consideration. This is safeguarded on Channels 3, 4 and 5 by the ITC's programme code, which requires for religious programmes a minimum of two hours a week for Channel 3, and an hour for Channel 4.

Although the BBC's Royal Charter does not contain any indication of a required quantity of religious programmes, it has always been understood that the BBC would provide a similar amount to that provided by Independent Broadcasting. The ITC will not, however, be able to influence *scheduling* for religious programmes as it can, for example, in the case of news and current affairs. So we should not be too sanguine about the future. If competition hots up in the broadcasting marketplace, experience tells me that audience ratings become a primary consideration and a dominant obsession for programme controllers.

The recent removal of the BBC's Daily Service to long wave on Radio 4, alongside other specialist programmes, is clearly an attempt to clear the decks before the three national commercial radio channels begin. TV-AM, the commercial breakfast channel, gives us another example. In its early days it took a rather relaxed view of its commitment to provide an element of religious affairs although this was rectified when the money started to roll in. All this means that the Churches must not be complacent and put all their eggs in the public service basket.

What are the advantages and disadvantages of the public service model for our communities of faith? On the positive side, religious faith and belief is celebrated, affirmed and explained at no cost to the Churches. Every week, Christians are seen and heard at worship. When the Archbishop of Canterbury appears on *Songs of Praise* or *Highway* he speaks to an audience, on a good day, of 6-7 million viewers. Research shows that 60% of the British population watches a religious programme in any given month. With an average Church attendance of 10% that means most of these are people who do not darken the doors of our churches on Sunday. The programmes are on the whole well-resourced and there is a good range of style and format - drama, documentary, outside broadcast, news and current affairs.

The fact that the Churches are seen as an integral part of a national public service broadcasting system is a recognition of the role of religion as a major cultural force in British society. As one speaker at the first Cranfield conference declared, we need a latter-day version of Descartes' maxim: "We are seen on the television, therefore we are". Furthermore, although the public service model means that the broadcasters have to ensure editorial impartiality and cannot be agents for particular interest groups, they do have a responsibility to meet the needs of these groups. This is reflected in the teaching series provided regularly on BBC1, and the Lent series organised by local radio in co-operation with the Churches.

So the public service system we have gives considerable advantages to the Churches. Even so, there are disadvantages. For many people one serious defect is the section of the ITC's code which forbids proselytising. To be fair, it is possible to invite viewers to write in for support literature in which recruitment of members is possible and where donations can be solicited. In the 1984 Billy Graham campaign, almost 10,000 wrote in after BBC and ITV broadcasts from Sunderland and Birmingham.

Even so, some Christians do feel they are in an unnecessary straitjacket. Also, because on television the amount of time allocated to religious programmes compared, say, with sport, is small (3% compared with 24% on BBC1 and 2) the mainstream Churches tend to dominate, and the smaller religious communities do not get much of a look in. Again, to be fair, there has been some improvement in recent years.

Another disadvantage is that because the broadcasters have editorial control, the Churches have little opportunity for influencing individual programmes. The Central Religious Advisory Committee has an important role influencing BBC and ITC religious broadcasting policy. Meeting as it does only twice a year, it cannot influence day-to-day programming. This means that the Churches' ability to influence those who represent them in individual programmes is very limited. The exception of course is local radio, both BBC and Independent. The Churches have a long track record in commercial radio where, for over 30 years, as with BBC local radio, local clergy and laity have been involved with the local religious output.

Now in the light of these pluses and minuses, what should our strategy be for the public service sector of broadcasting? In my view, the advantages far outweigh the disadvantages. But we should use the renewal of the BBC Charter in 1995 as the opportunity to press for more time to be devoted to religious programmes, particularly on BBC2. Individual churches need, as part of their own communication strategy, to provide the broadcasters with better information and stories and generally show more interest.

Under the 1990 Broadcasting Act, both the BBC and Channel 3 must allocate 25% of their output to independent programme makers. In this respect, Channel 4, as a publisher and commissioning agent broke the mould in 1984. Some Christian-based independents have already demonstrated that it is possible to have programmes transmitted on BBC television and Channels 3 and 4. The Churches Television and Radio Centre in Bushey, just outside London, has been very successful in this respect. Initially it will be independent Christians and the burgeoning independent churches who are best placed to take advantage of these opportunities for reasons I shall come to later.

However, it is important that the Churches develop a production strategy for this part of the broadcasting scene. The financial implications are daunting but the nettle will need to be grasped - and it will be later in the chapter. Where BBC and

Independent local radio is concerned, an infrastructure needs developing in conjunction with the Churches Advisory Council for Local Broadcasting, to develop resources for training and support for the continuing involvement of the Churches in local radio.

Now I turn my attention to what could be two major growth areas, local commercial radio and cable television. One projection suggests that Britain will have up to 400 local and community radio stations and the potential for up to 40 cable channels. The programme code for religious programmes on commercial local radio permits proselytising, provided it complies with the Broadcasting Act's requirement to be responsible, and does not improperly exploit the sensibilities of the listener, nor denigrate other people's religious beliefs. For television, the ITC code allows proselytising on specialist religious channels but not on general channels.

Since the public service obligations on commercial radio were lifted by the new Broadcasting Act, several stations have elbowed out the religious programming. In an increasingly competitive environment those religious groups who are able to offer programming material and pay for time will have a head-start, provided their material does not lose audiences or deter advertising. On LBC, the London radio station, the local Jewish programme is subsidised by the British Board of Jewish Deputies and sponsored by a local travel firm specialising in holidays in the Middle East. The religious affairs component on LBC is sponsored by the Bahai community. Because radio is much cheaper to produce than television, some Christian groups have already been involved.

But even here finance has been a determining factor. United Christian Broadcasters provided programmes from the Isle of Man but lack of money drove them off the airwaves. There is no question that the expertise is already available. GRF Christian Broadcasting, who last year won the Sandford St Martin major award in competition with BBC network radio, is already providing programming material for Radio Clyde in Glasgow. Some churches have also responded to the opportunities provided by the new community-radio licences. Wear FM in Sunderland in North East England is a community-radio station run on co-operative lines. The local Anglican deanery is a shareholder, together with the local polytechnic and borough council. The station is largely funded by grants from national and local government and from advertisements. In High Wycombe, a local ecumenical group is bidding for a community licence.

Initiative from the Churches at the local level is to be encouraged. In the past it has been left to individuals or para-Church groups. It was Fran Wildish who with fellow Christians took the initiative with the Vision Channel on cable television in Swindon. This channel is also available on other cable systems. Not surprisingly it is easier in some ways for individuals or para-Church groups to take initiatives than mainline Churches with their bureaucratic systems.

Coming from a theological tradition, where there is a strong emphasis on preaching that brings repentance and conversion, and an impatience with the constraints of public service religious broadcasting, the para-Church groups have responded quickly in other countries to develop a broadcast ministry. Because their style of worship and proclamation is lively, with popular music, and is focussed on a personality, they transfer easily and naturally to television.

Because these groups are virtually autonomous, they do not relate to nationally-structured Churches. This means that there is no control of personal ambition or accountability of any kind. The focus on a central authority figure is reinforced by television. This can lead to the development of a church of the airwaves. By using a persuasive style of proclamation which often appeals to individuals in a state of personal crisis, and yet which remains within the ITC's religious programme code, it would be possible to extract finance from viewers who can ill afford to be generous.

Because there is little contact between institutional Churches and, for example, the fast-growing house churches, or Restoration Churches as some of them are also called, and because we now live in a broadcasting system based on a market concept, it is inevitable that fortune will follow those who can respond quickly. It will also follow those who can also lay their hands on the cash necessary to get on the air, or at least for sufficiently long enough to establish an audience base which will support them. Faced with the opportunities of cable, and community and local radio, how should the mainstream Churches respond?

Leaving aside for the moment the question of finance there are two basic models for both commercial local radio and cable television. One possibility would be to provide a community-of-interest radio station which is religious. That is to say, apart from news bulletins, weather and local information, most of the programming, whether speech or music, would be religious. Similarly with cable (on the model of a specialist channel such as a sports channel or film channel) we establish a religious channel. This is a concept favoured by Janet Street-Porter, BBC's Head of Youth Programming.

The other model would be to apply for a local community radio licence and provide a mixed fare which would include a significant amount of religious material. In cable terms we follow the CBN model in the USA and provide a menu of programmes to suit all tastes, but with the emphasis on family viewing. In the case of a specialist radio station or cable channel, Christians would clearly go it alone, either as a denomination or ecumenically. With a general programme service the Church could go it alone or join a consortium or hitch a ride with whoever provides the service. Local circumstances would determine which route the Church adopted.

At first sight, there seems to be little future in the first option, devoted exclusively to wall-to-wall religion. In the first place, this option is only likely to attract viewers or listeners of similar interest. On the other hand, listeners may be prepared to pay in order to keep us on the air. The advantage of a general approach is that it will attract a much broader audience. It is also more likely to be attractive to a wider selection of advertisers and sponsors whose support will be essential.

There can be a positive aspect to a local cable channel or local radio predominantly devoted to religious material. Assuming a local diocese, deanery or church could afford to rent a cable channel, the church could use the channel to support its pastoral and teaching strategy. Because the church has complete editorial control it can develop programming to meet its overall pastoral and educational aims. If the local church cannot take on the responsibility it could be done by a religious order, like the Roman Catholic Order of St Paul which runs local TV stations in Italy.

Accepting that the target audience is Church members, spiritual needs can be met and developed, educational needs can be served and the sense of belonging to a Christian community can be reinforced. Support literature can be produced to supplement programmes of meditation, discussion, worship and talks. Religious magazine programmes and current affairs can be used to acquaint church members with what is happening in the wider Church. There would be opportunities for developing programmes geared to the needs of children, young people, families and the elderly. Because much of the programming can be done by volunteers, running costs could be controlled. The disadvantage is that the service I have described might be less than professional and compare unfavourably with other channels. It may also require a church to divert funding from other parts of its mission, unless additional finance can be raised either from members or from other sources.

It is not impossible for religious communities to take on the challenge of a national cable channel. The Southern Baptists in the USA have shown just how possible it is. The similarly named Interfaith VISN channels in the USA and the VISION Network in Canada also demonstrate the idea's viability. But the problems of running such a channel cannot be underestimated. Unlike the USA where there is a long history of the mainstream Churches and the religious orders producing programmes for the cable networks, Britain has no steady supply of Church-made programmes. Of course it would be possible to buy programmes to fill the schedule. Given the British distrust of foreigners, our even greater inadequacy to speak other languages and our aversion to subtitling, the major source would need to be the English-speaking areas of the world. However, it is not essential to provide a full daily schedule. In fact it is sensible to begin in a modest way, targetting a particular part of the day, at least at the beginning.

At present, cable reaches less than 10% of British homes. This is tiny compared even with the Republic of Ireland where 35% of homes can receive cable, let alone Belgium or Holland where 70-80% of homes are on cable networks. The projections for the expansion of British cable over the next 10 years are probably optimistic. In the 70s, the British government's interest in cable was based on its potential for developing a range of interactive services. Unfortunately, the cost in the early stage proved too heavy. Now, however, with the development of cable and satellite technology, the use of cable networks for telephone, home security, video conferencing, radio and home shopping, as well as for transmitting TV programmes, the prospects are more favourable.

It is clear to me that, at the present time, it would be impossible for an individual denomination to run a national cable channel. They might find it impossible to run a local channel. Unless the Churches are prepared to get together to provide a broad enough audience and subscriber-base, a national cable channel would certainly remain a pipe-dream. On an inter-faith basis, it becomes more viable, although working out an agreed policy could prove difficult. Even within the Christian community, the range and variety of doctrinal positions may prove an insurmountable problem.

But let's fly a kite. Let us suppose each paid-up member of the Christian Church was willing to subscribe a minimum of £10 per year to support a national channel. Based on MARC Europe figures for 1990, the following sums could be generated:

Church of England	£16m
Roman Catholic Church	£20m
Methodist Church	£5m
Baptist Church	£2.5m
United Reformed Church	£1.25m
Evangelical Alliance	£10m

If one included the Jews and the Muslims, a further £11 million could be provided. Of course, not every family would subscribe, some might be prepared to give more than £10, and subscriptions could be supplemented by sponsorship for individual programmes and by advertising revenue.

One of the important sets of questions which needs to be asked is what kind of programming would be provided and why? On the one hand a national cable channel could legitimately be used to meet the needs of the religious comnmunities. But on the other hand many would be keen to use such a channel to touch those outside communities of faith. There is also the wish among some Christians for a television service which above all provides wholesome fare without the level of violence, sex and bad language which some feel is present on the mainstream channels. It would not be impossible, of course, to draw up schedules which meet both sets of needs. In fact, on pragmatic grounds, it would be necessary to provide a service which offers a range of programming and to deliver a broad audience attractive to sponsors and advertising revenue.

This still leaves the question of sources for programmes. As I indicated earlier, the main sources would be English-speaking. We must not, however, overlook the growing potential of programme-making in Britain itself. Not only CTVC at Bushey, but increasingly other groups are developing video-making resources. The Salvation Army, the Church of Scotland, some of the house churches as well as individual dioceses and community groups have a growing library of programmes.

There is also increasing interest among European religious programme makers in co-production and co-funding ventures. The Co-Production Connection, an initiative of the European region of the World Association for Christian Communications (WACC) and the European Ecumenical Satellite Committee (EESC) provides a forum where producers can exchange information about programme plans. (See Chapter Eight.) One could be reasonably optimistic that a schedule could in fact be put together, initially for a limited number of hours each day. There would be a spine or core of programmes available nationally, but with the possibility of windows where local areas could opt out, and provide their own material.

A fascinating landscape is emerging in British broadcasting. In many respects it mirrors developments in other parts of Western Europe where there have been similar changes due to the same technological developments and the same deregulatory government policies. We need to preserve the best of what we already have in mainstream broadcasting and look positively at how we can take advantage of the new opportunities provided by local radio, and local and national cable television.

Because the main Churches in Britain, as in many other European countries, have received on the whole a good service from national broadcasters there has been little incentive for the Churches to develop an active interest in programme production. Even if they had been so interested, the cost is daunting. Ironically, the new opportunities for broadcasting arrive when most Churches are feeling the cold wind of recession. Although it is now much cheaper than it used to be to make broadcast-standard programmes, Churches would need to assess the claims of television and radio against their other commitments. Some, like the Church of Scotland, have already taken the plunge and upgraded their audio-visual facilities to broadcast standard. Inevitably, decisions will revolve around the question of whether we can afford it. The real question is can we afford not to? One thing is clear. If the main Churches do not get off their starting blocks, the autonomous independent congregations and Christian individualists most certainly will do so. Time is on our side - just.

Local Radio. As Churches we must concentrate first at the local level, building on what has already been achieved. Production standards need raising so they compare favourably with other parts of a local station's output. This means investing in training. The initial priority is to attend to the needs of BBC local radio, community radio and commercially-funded local radio. The local churches' presence needs re-inforcing and developing. At present there are no cohesive structures to address needs and opportunities.

What is needed in each area is an ecumenical group to monitor, support and develop Christian involvement. This already exists in some areas, particularly the counties of Hertfordshire and Bedfordshire and in the North East Broadcasting Council. These groups could provide resources, training and support where it did not exist, for current and potential radio producers and presenters. The Churches Advisory Council for Local Broadcasting could give assistance. The local group would maintain contact and interest with local radio stations on behalf of the wider Church.

Cable. If sufficient resources were available the group could also relate to local cable initiatives. At the local level there are already a number of video production units. The Church of England has video units in the dioceses of Blackburn, Coventry and Guildford. No doubt there are similar facilities in other Churches. There is, therefore, already in embryo a facility to address the needs of a local cable channel. We should also begin to explore the feasibility of a national cable channel by setting up a group representative of the Churches and other Christian groups. Seed money would be needed to conduct the feasibility study and draw up a business plan.

The Main Channels. We should support and feed religious broadcasting on the main channels. There is more to be gained by this than in expending energy on persuading government to pressurise the ITC to liberalise its ban on proselytising. The main channels give us access to major audiences. But we should begin, as a matter of urgency, to set up a group which is representative of all the Churches. This group must consider how, when cable is more fully developed, we might, as Churches, provide a cable channel - networked nationally - which would complement and extend what is already available on television. And we should not do separately what we ought to do together.

The Reverend Eric Shegog is Director of Communications for the General Synod of the Church of England.

XII

John P. Foley

Catholic Europe

There are tremendous opportunities in radio. In Portugal, a Catholic radio network, Radio Renasçenca, is the most popular radio voice in the nation with two programme services and a strong presence both in medium-wave and FM, with a short-wave service aimed at Brazil and Africa. Radio Renasçenca, which survived a Marxist takeover attempt during the revolution of the 1970s, is now interested in launching a Catholic television channel.[11]

In Spain, another Catholic radio network, COPE, is also the most popular radio voice in the country, yet with a strong national service based in Madrid supplemented by local programming from diocesan affiliates.

In both Portugal and Spain, the Catholic networks offer not only religious and devotional programming, but also respected news programmes and popular music and talk shows. The administrators of both networks judge it essential to offer a broad mix of programming to attract a wide audience and, therefore, to assure financial viability. Some critics charge that the networks are not "Catholic" enough, but the response is offered that the networks seek not only to save the saved but to reach out to those who may not be active in the practice of their religion, and also to provide a self-sustaining broadcast service which does not depend on a Church subsidy.

In Holland, there are at least three religious programming services among the groups allowed to broadcast in a truly unique system of communications organisation. Among the programming services identified as religious, the Catholic KRO is the most popular, and it too offers religious, cultural and entertainment programming. As the mainline Protestant programming service now has a fundamentalist competitor, there were those who wished to start a more conservative Catholic programming service, because they felt that KRO was perhaps too tolerant of dissident views within the Catholic Church. No such alternative programme service has been started, but it is said that KRO has perhaps become more moderate in tone, possibly to avoid offering a motive for a Catholic competitor to enter the field.

In Italy, France and Belgium, Catholic radio stations of a more devotional type are becoming more widespread and more active. These stations do not have the wide audience of their Catholic but less devotional counterparts in Portugal, Spain and Holland, but they do have a devoted following.

In Eastern Europe, as privatization even of the media is contemplated, the Catholic Church, which possesses few material resources in most countries and which had little or no access to the formerly Communist-controlled media, is faced with many challenges. First, the Church must seek access for religious programming (on) networks which are still state-controlled and still staffed by personnel from the former regime. Second, the Church must prepare Catholics for communications activity to which they had previously been denied both access and training. Finally, the Church must articulate a policy regarding future private broadcasting opportunities.

In Poland, a religious department has been established in the state radio and television network. In Hungary, few new radio initiatives have been launched by the Church, but it has sought to establish a presence on television. In Lithuania, the Church has been able to gain access to both radio and television stations, but many religious programme tapes were destroyed when some Soviet soldiers sacked the television station.

What should be the posture of the Catholic Church in Europe regarding broadcasting opportunities in the 1990s?

First, it would seem essential to maintain or to establish a good relationship with existing broadcast entities, both in radio and television, because all media should recognise and serve the religious and spiritual needs of their listeners. The collapse of Marxist regimes in the East has made clear that a failure to recognise human spiritual values can create widespread resentment and that there is a hunger not only for material opportunity and political liberty but also for religious freedom.

The relationship with existing broadcasting entities should include not only a willingness to co-operate in the production of specifically religious programming of both a devotional and public service nature, but also an openness to be available for news and public affairs programmes. An active engagement with the creative community which prepares dramatic and other entertainment programming is also needed to insure that Christian values are known and respected.

Second, where possible, stations under Catholic or even ecumenical auspices should be maintained or started. Christians often have a need for means of communication independent of public or other private broadcast stations to guarantee that the Christian message or the Church's teaching may reach the general public without the filter of a secular news or broadcast organisation.

The philosophy of these stations will differ from nation to nation. In some they may provide a broad spectrum of programming, as in Portugal, Spain and Holland. In others they may choose a more devotional approach, directing their message to a specific segment of the listening audience with a profound interest in continuous religious programming. In the former case, support from commercial sponsorship is often sufficient to maintain the broadcast effort; in the latter case, it is often necessary to solicit funding from listeners or from other benefactors or to seek a Church subsidy.

In television, the international Catholic communications organisations for radio and television (*Unda*) and for cinema and audiovisuals (OCIC) have been seeking to make programming available through interchange, but this is not always easy in a multilingual and multicultural continent. Lumen 2000, the Catholic movement which seeks to evangelize through radio and television, has also made available programming (especially of a magazine nature) which can easily be dubbed in many languages.

In any case, the work of the international Catholic communications organisations can be most important in arranging professional training, in providing a forum for the interchange of ideas and for providing an opportunity for co-operation across the entire continent.

Pope John Paul II has called for a re-evangelization of the European continent and has emphasised the Christian roots of European culture. For Catholics, both these emphases should be priorities for the 1990s.

The disappearance of the imposed unity of Marxist ideology in the East and the erosion of spiritual values through rampant consumerism in the West mean that all parts of the continent need to be reminded of the religious and spiritual source of European culture and of the spiritual basis of human dignity and of natural human rights, all of which have their source in God.

The spiritual hunger of many in the East and the spiritual emptiness of many in the West truly indicate the need for a new evangelization; the creative presentation of the good news of Christ in an attractive and compelling, but non-threatening manner. Faith is the most precious treasure of a Christian, and it paradoxically increases and deepens as it is shared. Words - and images - of faith, of hope and of love are needed on radio and television in all societies so that the people of Europe may have an opportunity to appreciate their dignity as children of God and as citizens of a civilization which bears the name Christian.

John P. Foley, titular Archbishop of Neapolis, is an American. He is the President of the Pontifical Council for Social Communications.

XIII

Nils-Gøran Wetterberg

Lutheran Sweden

In 1924 the clergy said that the churches would be emptied. Why? Because in that year the Church of Sweden started to broadcast regular Sunday services over the radio. In 1930 people feared that the new theatres would be emptied. Why? Because in that year the sound-track movie was introduced and people could see plays on movies instead of in theatres. In 1955 it was said that now the cinema would be emptied because from now on people would sit in their homes and watch films on TV. The theatres were not emptied. The cinemas were not emptied. The churches were not emptied!

New media have always been met with scepticism. Even the great reformer Martin Luther was met with scepticism when the Bible was translated into languages that were understood by people other than the clergy. But Luther was far-sighted and very soon recognised the power and use of modern media. He believed that "Now that Gutenberg has invented the art of printing we have got the means to defeat the Pope." In this ecumenical era we don't agree with him on that point but we do try to use modern media to spread the Gospel of Jesus Christ. And we know for certain that the media of today are the most efficient means to transmit ideas, thoughts and opinions and perhaps to change attitudes. The Church is surrounded by media. She should not be an isolated part of the world but right in the middle of it.

In 1979 a major breakthrough occurred in the Swedish media world. Many features within the state monopoly for radio broadcasting expired. Local radio was introduced for a test period and 16 local stations started to broadcast. Local radio became permanent in 1985. Six years later, more than 156 transmitters had been established.

The Church of Sweden is represented in more than 125 of these stations. Behind all these programmes are several thousand volunteers working as producers and technicians. Local radio has become part of the activities of many parishes. In the beginning there was something amateur about local radio but over the years it has developed into a professional service. Many parishes have their own full-time employees for the radio activity. Local radio has become part of our conscious strategy for spreading the Gospel and an important part of the total activities of the Church.

The state monopoly for TV transmission came to an end in 1986 with the introduction of local cable TV. As with local radio, cable TV is allowed for associations, clubs and churches. This is all in a non-commercial context. Commercial advertising is not allowed.

Television is an adventurous medium and as such it can promote the message of the Church. Our message cannot be transmitted through the written word only. Primarily it is transmitted through people. Television may be the medium for transmitting opinions and personal conviction, reinforced with moving pictures.

Cable TV has one great advantage in comparison to regional and national television. It's close to the viewer! The surroundings are well-known and recognisable. The people who participate are well-known - perhaps even old acquaintances. My message tends to be more important when I personally know the man or woman who presents it. It touches me in a way that regional or national television cannot touch me. The more that viewers are aware that the message comes in the context of their own reality the greater the possibility that the message will be effective.

The local-TV viewer can believe that he has an influence on the medium - and he has. It is easy to get in contact with the station.

The producer is local. What is shown concerns my town and my surroundings. The programmes may cover just about anything from reports and interviews on local activities to discussions on various local topics; street violence, social activities, the theatre. Christian cable TV should show that the churches are a part of the local community and reflect a true engagement with society. Today cable TV is present in 18 towns in Sweden and Christians are involved in every place. The Church of Sweden broadcasts in 9 of the 18 towns.

The motive to broadcast on local television is the same as for local radio. The Church of Sweden makes use of the media to reach those we cannot reach by ordinary channels. We try to reach those who are not regular churchgoers or take part in the various activities of the church. Through radio and television we try to tell them about our opinions and activities. We try to explain what we think and what we believe in. The person-to-person meeting has to be the foundation for bringing about the experience of the Christian faith. Television and radio cannot bring about salvation but they can show people the fruits of faith and arouse interest and curiosity in the Christian message. But, unlike the national broadcasting company, we do not broadcast church services.

Today, every local broadcasting organisation pays for its own costs. Advertising and sponsorship are not allowed. The law limits the number of broadcasting organisations considerably. Only those who have the financial possibility can broadcast, and it is expensive. We use the media to bring about knowledge of the Church and the views of the Church on events in our world.

Commercially-interested parties are lining up for their place in the new media but it is equally important for the message of the Church to be heard - of that we are sure. Local broadcasting by cable TV is expensive but Sweden is now seriously discussing the possibility of admitting advertising in the national channels and - if this becomes a reality - there is the hope that advertising may also be admitted on both local radio and television. If this should happen it will solve part of the financial problem and lead to rapid growth of local television stations all over the country. One way to finance the broadcasting of local TV programmes is to transmit Text TV. Various local organisations, theatres and municipal authorities broadcast text information to the people who live in their area. The sending organisations pay a fixed fee-per-page and the money helps to finance part of local television's production costs.

Cable TV is primarily intended for densely-populated areas. Rural areas will probably have to wait a long time for their own service. After its introduction through a parliamentary decision in 1986, local TV has slowly become established in the areas where there has been serious and goal-conscious planning. In 1987 the Church of Sweden began a test project in order to test the effectiveness of permanent, regular programmes. After three years the Church can claim the following achievements:

1. The Church of Sweden now has a full-time producer and project-leader as well as part-time technical personnel.

2. Weekly programmes have been produced and distributed by cable TV for the Malmö area in the south of Sweden. The series is called Meeting Place (Moteplats).

3. An Advent calendar - 28 episodes - has been produced and distributed. This is the only programme of its kind that has been produced outside the state TV company.

4. The experience of this test period has been shared with a large number of people within the Church, especially in those regions where local television is on the march. The experience has also been made known to a large number of people at our annual Media Convention and at special district TV conventions.

5. Extensive courses for future producers and technicians have been held in the Church's television centre in Malmö along with seminars for decision-makers. Courses have been held for preachers who volunteer to lead services on television.

For centuries the Church has worked hard to invite people to communion and service to spread the Gospel of Jesus Christ - to meet him. Traditionally this meeting takes place in the church. But nowadays it does not only happen there. It is not enough to ring the church bells and hope that people will come along. We simply must make use of every means and medium available for us. An important part of evangelism is to tell people about the Christian faith and to explain what the Church means. For, as Ingmar Lindqvist, the Finnish theologian and media researcher, puts it, to be excluded from modern media is practically the same as to be non-existent.

Nils-Gøran Wetterberg is responsible for all matters concerning radio, film and TV in the Church of Sweden.

XIV

Renato Maiocchi

Protestant Italy

Regular radio broadcasting started in Italy in 1910. But the first Protestant voice on radio went on the air only 34 years later, in 1944. And it took an army for it to be heard! Rome was under Allied rule and, in order to get access to radio, a Protestant minister called upon the Commander-in-Chief. As the Allies advanced, this example was followed by other Protestants in other regions. After the war there were Protestant Radio programmes in Rome, Geneva, Turin, Milan, Venice and Trieste.

In 1951, when the national network was restored, the strictly-Catholic Christian Democratic Party took an elegant decision: the 15-minute Protestant programme was allocated to 6 am on Sunday mornings. The situation improved in 1968, when the programme was lengthened to 20 minutes and began at the later Sunday morning time of 7.35. It could now include a news magazine as well as radio worship. Protestants continued to consider the broadcasting time as too early but nowadays 7.35 on Sunday morning proves to be a very good time for radio in general, and for public radio particularly. So in Protestant circles the present situation is considered adequate.

Regular television programmes started in 1954. Here too Protestants were excluded. Discussions began in 1968 but the first results were only achieved in 1973 when the first-ever Protestant TV programme went on air, together with the first-ever Jewish programme. The two programmes were broadcast in total isolation - in the afternoon on a channel where at that time there were no other programmes either. The situation today can be summarized as follows:

Radio: Protestants have 20 minutes every Sunday morning at 7.35 on Radio One.

Television: Protestants and Jews each have a 30-minute programme every second week. These are on Sunday evenings on *RAIDUE* and begin officially at 11.30pm.

Protestants are reasonably satisfied with their situation on radio and fairly dissatisfied about the television situation.

PLUS POINTS

1. Both the radio and TV programmes are broadcast by RAI but produced by the Federation of Protestant Churches in Italy. This is the only case of its kind within RAI. It is an acknowledgement by RAI that in the Italian cultural context it would be impossible to channel the voice of religious minorities through radio and TV without involving them in the production.

2. RAI pays a fixed amount to the Federation of Protestant Churches for every production. The amount is not great but leaves Protestants with the tasks of: a) inventing cheap but effective productions; b) seeking co-operation with brethren everywhere especially in the field of valuable international productions or co-productions; c) economising on certain occasions in order to invest more at other times. Above all, this system gives us limited resources but full freedom not only in terms of content but also in terms of operational freedom. Within our resources we can produce anything, anywhere, whenever we wish, without depending on RAI. If RAI wanted to censor a programme, this would involve censoring the Federation of Protestant Churches. This would be much easier than censoring the Vatican but harder than censoring the producer.

MINUS POINTS

1. While our radio programme has a very good broadcasting time our TV programme is officially broadcast at 11.30 pm on Sunday evenings. In reality it often goes on air at around 12

midnight and sometimes even later. This is not as tragic as it might be in other social and cultural contexts, because in Italy even after our programme the TV continues. It is the time for cultural programmes. We don't dislike that. But we have only this one window and the Italian religious, social, political and cultural scene has been defended for centuries from all possible influences of non-Catholic Christianity. Expulsion, exile, persecution and at best ostracism, discrimination and marginalisation have been - up to some 20 years ago - the rule. Therefore into that single window we cannot pour only culture. We have to pour Bible, history, devotion, Protestants, events and ecumenical news and views. So our fortnightly appointment on television is somewhat narrow.

2. The allocation of specific broadcasting time for religious minorities, entrusted as it is to bodies representing such minorities, has a possible negative side: the public-broadcasting system considers that it has thus fulfilled its duty to secure a pluralistic presentation in the religious field. It tends to be impermeable to our news and events in the rest of the output. In other words the airtime allocated to religious minorities serves as an alibi to the age-old Italian habit of identifying Christianity with Catholicism. If you look for the journalist who deals with religious information in the national news media, you must know him by his job designation: The Vaticanist.

But we do not complain too much. Our problem is not so much better broadcasting time or more resources. Our main problem is to contribute to a change of mentality, to a real pluralism, to a genuine modernisation in this part of our country's life. At a time when other religious cultures are already more and more a part of our nation, this struggle is no longer just a struggle for our own rights. But, of course, we also need to adjust our own goal: less use of radio and TV as right-of-access and more use of the media as a service to the public.

Renato Maiocchi works as a television producer with the Federazione delle Chiese Evangeliche in Italia. He became Chief Producer in 1988. He is a Baptist lay preacher.

XV

Wim Koole

The Co-Production Connection[12]

Co-production is not new but it is still rare in the religious broadcasting field. Up till now only bilateral projects have had a good chance of success. Nevertheless, shortfalls in production budgets make co-production an increasingly important option for survival. International co-operation gives more prestige and support to programme themes that may be critical or controversial. In a period where religion is becoming less connected with political power there is more freedom for this international exchange. It can be helpful to introduce people to other ways of reflecting on religious convictions. But, co-production of religious programmes raises extra complications compared with co-operation in children's, youth or sports programmes. One aspect of international co-operation in the television profession is that initiatives are still very much dependent on mutual friendship and confidence.

The history of religious television on our continent is nearly exclusively related to public television. The funding of staff and of the total costs of programmes was taken for granted by the public stations. However more and more limitations are now imposed. Increasing secularism makes the security of religious departments less self-evident. More expensive projects can no longer be realised without co-producing partners. A religious BBC series on grass-roots Christianity (filmed in far away places like Brazil, China, South Korea) can only be produced

104

with the financial co-operation of North American and Australian companies.

Formerly the traditionally-strong position of religion in national broadcasting made it unnecessary to co-produce. Co-production happened only incidentally and as a result of friendship and mutual confidence between colleagues. Initiatives were tried, often with idealistic intentions. Too often there were disappointments. Some years ago - when the ideal of European unity came to the surface - strong partners with long experience, the religious departments of BBC and WDR (Cologne) together with IKON (Netherlands), made several attempts to start a European Television Magazine on current religious affairs. The plan did not get off the ground. The time was not yet ripe.

Religion is very deeply rooted in regional and national culture. That makes it an interesting subject, but also makes it very difficult to communicate in the casual visual context of television, especially when the audience is less related to the culture of the programme. I remember well some discussions we had about trying to explain in this magazine programme the disobedience of the Dutch Calvinist fishermen towards the fishing limitations ordered by the European Community. We wished to make the explanation to the Dutchmen's Portuguese fishermen colleagues. The roots of belief, convictions, moral dilemmas are strongly related to regional traditions and emotional persuasion. What seemed on first hearing a good idea for co-production between colleagues who had known each other for many years had to be discussed intensely on a theological level - before we could start.

Religion is well-known as a possible source of emotional conflicts. I have always believed that this is the reason why the European Broadcasting Union has until recently refused to create a working group for religious programmes along the lines of their longstanding groups for drama, sports and children's programmes. This is understandable. But, despite its contrasts and conflicts, religion is a dramatic subject and suitable for television. However, for the very same reason it is a complicated theme to discuss between co-producing partners.

In the planning of co-production in comedy, fiction, children's and youth programmes, one can avoid documentaries, disputes on moral or exegetical details. When dealing with religion this dialogue seems inescapable. This can be an interesting aspect, but it demands time and patience, two qualities not-too-abundantly available in our profession.

In spite of those historical problems I have reasons for believing in the future of co-produced religious programmes in Europe. Weaknesses can be turned into strengths. Religious television has a narrow tradition as far as television programme categories are concerned. Information has taken the lion's share. Education has played a minor part. TV drama and fiction in general are nearly-missing genres. A real shortcoming is the lack of programmes for children. The Church with her long tradition of education should be represented on television with the continuing story of Old and New Testaments and the history of Christianity. In earlier times sales departments of public broadcasting companies sold production kits. Music, drawings and other illustrations of short stories for children were made available on videotape. The presentation of the translated and -if necessary - revised script could be presented in a variety of languages. This way of making good material available is still a good concept. It can make production easier in many countries and enable colleagues to add their national flavour to the programme.

Recently in all Central and Eastern European countries transmission time on television has been made available for religious programmes. As well as the broadcasting of worship, there will be great demand for TV magazines with a variety of information on church and religious life, a means to catch up on the lack of information. A TV magazine is one of the more expensive programme formats. A regular well-organised exchange of news items would be of great help.

Worship in its liturgical, meditational format is still an important means of representing religion on television. Liturgy and meditation still have a high value for millions of people. They feed the memory of the sources of life that are too easily neglected in our society. Protestant colleagues can feel a little envy that the Pope with his pilgrimages and his appearances on festival days is such a regular Roman Catholic in our homes. At an international workshop on television worship[13] a plan was put forward to create a more regular ecumenical tradition for the exchange of worship services via Eurovision. An older plan to have an annual Pentecost service produced for transmission in many countries will only get off the ground if the responsibility is given to a central co-production institution capable of taking initiatives.

Co-production can be arranged in many different ways. One way is to share part of the production budget or by offering a pre-sale contract to the producer. This is the easiest way of co-operation but one has to be convinced of the qualities of the producer. Then there is a literal exchange of programmes. These are produced by each of the partners on the same theme or subject. The slogan is: Make one and get four in return! At first sight this approach appears easier than it turns out to be in reality. Extra costs and much time are taken up in the preparation of such projects involving directors and producers from several countries. There is an absolute need for partners to tune in to the ideas of the other members. There has to be a strong will to work together with respect. But these co-productions can be set up without any exchange of money. All financial and legal aspects are home-based. The exchange of rights is exclusively organised on a bilateral basis. Both the challenge and the problem of earlier co-productions was to give them a real European character.

The weakening of the traditional Church institutions in European society is not only a disadvantage. It opens chances for a more open-minded view of religion. When religion becomes more and more a spiritual phenomenon and is freed from hierarchical and dogmatic pressure it can develop once more into a fascinating dimension of human life. Television is the outstanding example of a medium capable of sustaining this trend. Rules and principles will not dominate - values and standards will. They are much more capable of reflection in fantasy and drama. There will be less of the monologue of the sermon and more discussion and dialogue, the main elements of the talkshow. The tendency in international public broadcasting to create more assignments for independent producers can create a new international scope for the development of religious programmes.

Wim Koole was director of IKON, the Dutch religious programme production house. He now co-ordinates the Hilversum-based Co-Production Connection, which is sponsored by the European Ecumenical Satellite Committee.

XVI

David W. Clark

The Public Interest

Do the new opportunities for religious broadcasting run counter to public interest standards?

The "public interest" was defined early on in the regulation of broadcasting in the United States. The phrase "public interest, convenience, and necessity" was part of the Communications Act of 1934. This was the standard laid down by Congress to guide the Federal Communications Commission in regulating broadcasting in areas where the act had no specific provisions. The FCC was seen as a fiduciary acting to regulate broadcasting in the public's interest.[14] In 1946 the FCC gave more specific definition to station operators' public service requirements in the famous "Blue Book" (so-called because of the colour of the covers) which required: that stations carry some "sustaining" or free programmes; that stations produce live locally-originated programmes; that there be some discussion of public issues and that there be no excessive advertising.[15] It was the requirement that stations provide sustained programming that afforded the opportunity for the churches to provide religious programming.

The PSB ideal developed along somewhat different lines in Britain, where the BBC became the model under Sir John Reith's autocratic direction from 1927 to 1938. It came to consist of the following elements:[16]

1. A public corporation which is insulated from either commercial or political pressures. Financial independence ensured through receiver licence fees which provide a secure revenue source.

2. Rural dwellers as well as their more easily-reached urban counterparts are accorded broadcast service, as are the minorities in the population.

3. Programme producers are given artistic and creative freedom within broad boundaries.

4. Programming represents a variety of formats. It also seeks to attain political balance.

The BBC's programming philosophy of giving a lead reflected Reith's view that broadcasting content should be ahead of the popular taste at least some of the time. It should reflect "the best in every department of human knowledge, endeavour and achievement."[17] This rather prescriptive perspective of the role of broadcasting in society has been practised in many of the countries who, following the British lead, adopted the public service model of broadcasting.

The PSB model assumes that there are prudent and even-handed broadcasting regulators who act as fiduciaries for the public. Inherent in this model is the assumption that these regulators will turn to programmers who are trustworthy, competent, fair and in some sense representative of the main viewpoints within the population on a given topic. They take upon themselves to determine not just what the audience wants but what they believe the audience ought to see or hear. Thus the regulators and programmers assume a very powerful gate-keeper role for audiences. Today, in Britain and in other nations who have adopted this prescriptive (at times some would say coercive) programming philosophy there are pressures for change.

PUBLIC SERVICE SHORTCOMINGS AND PRESSURES FOR CHANGE

There are several reasons why change is being called for. Foremost is the competition for audiences. Reith conceived of the BBC as having a monopoly on broadcasting and thus able

110

to control the choices available to the audience. This changed for television in Britain in 1955 and the BBC was eventually required to launch another channel which could compete successfully for audience with ITV, the new commercial network. Finances are yet another source of pressure for change. Licence fees which once provided an adequate, if not ample, source of funding have proven inadequate in recent years as the costs of producing programming has risen steadily. This has forced public service broadcasters to turn to the government or commercial interest for additional funds. In so doing they have become more beholden to the two centres of power from which they have so assiduously sought to remain independent in the past.

There have also been charges that PSB systems produce programming which is not really representative of the various shades of opinion within the population. The contention is that the PSB gatekeepers, in the name of giving a lead, have allowed programming to assume a certain predictable liberal cant and at times an admittedly biased viewpoint. The PSB producers' response is that they are not interested in representing every minority interest in society but only those issues which are central to human life such as the arts, religion and public policy. Religion and its function in society is what is significant. From this perspective any religion is as good as any other. Christianity is not to be accorded any more standing than Islam.

The charge of bias in PSB is raised about various kinds of programming including, by evangelical broadcasters, religious programming. There is history in the US to support this contention. As the radio and television networks developed in the 1920s they made available sustained or donated time each week for religious broadcasting as part of their public service obligation. The networks deferred to the National Council of Churches to supply Protestant programming. The NCC selected the mainline denominations to produce these programmes. During the 1930s and 40s this denominational programming demonstrated what evangelicals felt was a consistent liberal theological bias.

This is not surprising since the liberal theology had been embraced by the leaders of most mainline denominations. With

111

the exception of an occasional programme produced by the Missouri Lutherans only Protestants who were theologically liberal were give access to this free network time. Roman Catholic Bishop Fulton J. Sheen with the prime-time TV programme *Life Is Worth Living* probably represented orthodox Christianity better than the programming produced by the NCC. This may be one reason it drew very large audiences.

The result was that evangelicals such as Charles E. Fuller, were forced to buy time for their programmes. The cost of purchasing such time was high and these broadcasters developed an infrastructure to raise the funds needed to stay on the air. Once local stations realized that the time they were donating to the networks could be sold to evangelical broadcasters they began to make time available. Initially only marginal stations sold time but gradually most network affiliates in both radio and TV sold time for religion.

As more time was sold, less sustained time was available and the mainline church programmes could no longer be heard or seen.[18] Certainly the mainline denominations had the resources to make such purchases but they seemed to lack the resolve necessary to produce and finance nationally-syndicated programmes. The marketplace gradually pushed out the religious programme producers who were unable or unwilling to buy airtime. After a while local radio and television stations carrying a majority of religious programming became available to Christian broadcasters.

National Religious Broadcasters was organized in 1942 by evangelicals who were forced to buy time. A primary concern of the organization was, and still is, insuring that access to purchase time for religious broadcasting be maintained. With over 800 institutional members, the NRB today represents a majority of all Protestant religious programmers and stations in America. The NRB estimated in 1990 there were over 1,400 radio and 200 television stations that might be classified as mainly "religious" in programming orientation. If the gatekeepers of the National Council of Churches had been more open in allowing evangelical access to airtime the NRB might not have been needed. From the perspective of the evangelicals, their systematic exclusion by liberal religious gatekeepers in the name of the public service raises doubts about whether such a system of centralized control such as once existed in the US can be made responsive to the broad range of religious viewpoints represented in a population.

There are those who contend that the religious programming produced by the BBC and ITV is not representative of the religious diversity in Britain. More specifically they claim that the same systematic exclusion of evangelical Christians which occurred in the US until the 1960s has characterized British religious broadcasting until the present. Eric Shegog, the director of communications for the Church of England, points out the emphasis in religious television shifted in the important area of evangelism from the 1960 Pilkington Committee recommendations, in which one objective was to reach those outside the churches, to the 1977 Central Religious Advisory Committee, when the objective changed to "meeting the religious interests, concerns and needs of those outside the churches."[19] He notes that: "Unlike the American paid-time religious programmes, therefore, religious programmes in the United Kingdom have taken account of the liberal tradition and been reluctant to preach."[20]

But for evangelical Christians the requirement that they not confront the audience with the claims of Christ through preaching strikes at the heart of their understanding of the Christian faith. It appears that the requirements laid down for religious programming resulted in the de facto elimination of evangelicals, even within the mainline churches, from having access to broadcasting in Britain. The Broadcasting Act of 1990 opens access to cable and local radio for religious broadcasting. Andrew Quicke, a former VisNews producer, has written on the regulations dealing with religion in this new legislation.[21] It may provide some opportunities for the marginalized evangelicals and charismatics, as well as other groups, to have limited access to audiences. Shegog notes that the fastest-growing religious groups are the evangelical house churches and the black Pentecostals.[22]

But it appears that the Independent Television Commission through various regulatory procedures, will continue to exclude programming from such groups from ITV. One reason given is the fear of an invasion by American televangelists. Fears of such an invasion seem greatly exaggerated in the light of the apparently different preferences of British audiences and the impossibility of raising financial support to fund airtime. Yet this somewhat irrational fear of an American "invasion", as it has been called in the British press, should not be the basis for eliminating indigenous evangelicals with a desire to utilize broadcasting in evangelism.

THE IMPACT OF NEW BROADCASTING OPPORTUNITIES

One lesson is clear in viewing the development of religious broadcasting. It will thrive only in a symbiotic relationship with the secular broadcasting establishment. Some developments may be harmful to it while others will promote growth in religious audiences. The 1990s will bring significant changes to broadcasting in Europe. Some of these will have a direct impact on religious broadcasting.

New delivery systems and new technology by the year 2000 will allow access to a greater number of religious publics at a significantly lower cost. As cable, DBS, wireless cable, HDTV, digital radio and other technologies move into the marketplace they will displace some of the previous delivery systems but typically they then attract new viewers/listeners. More and more broadcasting will become narrowcasting.

An example of the way this might work is in the Assemblies' of God use of television to bring coverage of the biennial church council to its members in the US and overseas. In the past they have bought time on several cable networks such as CBN's Family Channel for a live 2-hour programme. Churches installed special receiver and projection equipment so that they could join in as participants in the service. Several live feeds from remote locations in the US and overseas were included. Those who could not attend a local church were advised what cable channels would carry the programme and those with home satellite dishes were told of the satellite and channel. Some local television stations also carried the programme. Those who could not see the live presentation at all were told where to obtain a videotape of the programme. The response to this programme was positive and those in the pew were made to feel a part of a worship service at a conference that typically

114

only their pastor and one lay person was ever able to attend. There was also a certain amount of status conferral on the church leadership simply because of the television coverage.

Another example is the pilot programme using satellite, cable and video cassette to distribute news and prayer bulletins to 100 churches in Britain. This research project is sponsored by the Evangelical Alliance, Tear Fund and the Evangelical Missionary Alliance. Before technical difficulties emerged, the $2^1/_2$-hour pilot programmes had previously been aired on the Olympus satellite. Initial reaction to the programme looks promising.[23] This combining of over-the-air, cable, DBS and videocassettes suggests the kind of hybrid delivery systems we will see more of in the years ahead.

Programming production equipment will also continue to decrease in cost and complexity so that even relatively-small religious organizations will be able to equip themselves to produce technically competent television programmes. At the 1991 National Association of Broadcasters in Las Vegas new developments in Hi8, SVHS and an amazing digital effects generator which costs about 15% of its nearest competitor demonstrated these possibilities. For about $30,000 it is possible to set up a complete production unit which will produce air quality TV programmes. Inevitably, it seems to me, such production capability will create pressure for more access to audiences. The centralized control of religious programming in the public service model will be more and more challenged by groups with the capability to produce programmes that at least some audiences will want to see or hear. *(See pp. 136-48)*

Another development which will place greater pressure on centralised programming control is the availability of the local station or local cable channel. In the US the majority of all religious programmes are made by the local stations, not by the nationally-syndicated televangelists. Every local religious station has a daily chat show or teaching or music programme. Thus, literally thousands of local programmes are produced and aired daily in religious radio and television stations. Because the producers have a better understanding of local spiritual needs, they no doubt command a much larger combined audience than the national programmes.

A consequence is more audience response and financial support.In Europe, Italy may be the model for local Christian radio and television. Such localism will offer opportunities to previously marginalised groups such as the evangelicals and charismatics and represents a threat to the prescriptive central-ised control of religious programming by the mainline churches in the PSB system. One complicating element of such localism in Europe is the emergence of nationalistic and ethnic agendas which, combined with religious fervor, could form programmes essentially political or ethnic in appeal and intent.

Yet another development which will have an impact on PSB religious programming is the emergence of indigenous religious media leaders. Until now, televangelists have been thought of as an American phenomenon, seeking to impose their minis-tries on other cultures. But with media exposure there is nothing to prevent the rise of charismatic indigenous media personalities. Some have suggested that Europeans have been somehow inoculated against such personalities. I doubt this will prove to be the case. The combination of personality, ethnic, linguistic and religious appeal will doubtless produce such media leaders in the coming decade in Europe.

With the promised EEC policy of television without frontiers it may be impossible to isolate the influence of a European televangelist. Europeans may actually emerge with significantly more influence than their American counterparts. After all one country recently elected a playwright to its presidency. Given the reluctance of most governments to regulate religion overtly it is fair to wonder to whom such leaders will be accountable. Is not now the time for those currently involved in religious broadcasting to begin building the structures of accountability?

Many forces, including the new opportunities and technology, are acting on the PSB systems to bring about change. In the area of religious programming the main problem has been that the many religious groups, including those which show the greatest vitality, have been marginalised by a system which prescribes the appropriate doses and content of religious programming. For the few religious broadcasters who have had access it has been a unique opportunity to present religious programming at little or no cost. The claim by PSB proponents that such prescriptive programming respects the dignity of the viewer and listener carries in it the implication that the audience is somehow unable or unwilling to make appropriate selections of what they wish to see or hear. Such derogatory views of the audience by all-knowing gatekeepers have already been swept aside in much of Eastern Europe by waves of democracy. Can the PSB systems of Western Europe stand against this rising tide of audience access to the media? I think not. Perhaps a PSB system like that of Holland which allows access to time and resources based on religious membership would be an effective compromise between a totally commercial system and the current restrictive PSB systems of Western Europe.

David W. Clark is Dean of the College of Communication and the Arts of Regent University, Virginia Beach. Since 1977, he has been associated with CBN, the Christian Broadcasting Network founded by the Television Evangelist Pat Robertson. Dr. Clark is now the President of National Religious Broadcasters (NRB).

XVII

Jim McDonnell

I Believe in Public Service Broadcasting

One of the urgent tasks of the Christian churches in Europe today is to offer the possibility of integration of personhood and wholeness of spirit to people who are living in culturally and socially fragmented and incoherent societies. A major factor in the promotion of this cultural fragmentation is the unrelenting bombardment of diverse and contradictory messages from the mass media. In a media-saturated society people find increasing difficulty in making sense of all the messages they receive and of bringing them together into a coherent vision of life.

At the heart of the modern media, including broadcasting, is a vacuum of meaning and in this the media are faithful reflectors of modern society. In the place of shared meanings is a multitude of opinions and behaviours. The danger is that the centrifugal forces of modernity so evident in television and other media will propel us into a future in which the medium of public discourse will be the advertising slogan and the "sound bite". In the words of Rabbi Jonathan Sacks, in his recent Reith lectures, we live in a society in which a variety of social changes, including the growth and diversity of the media, have undermined "our sense of being part of a single moral community in which very different people are brought together under a canopy of shared values".

Christians have the task of resisting this process and, however haltingly, working to strengthen those elements in society which bring people together rather than drive them further apart. In Britain, the exaltation of private experience and private interest above common understanding and public good has intensified and exaggerated social divisions and strains in the past decade. The broadcast media have both reflected this process and been its victims insofar as political, commercial and technological pressures have conspired to undermine established public broadcasting and to accelerate the growth in specialized programmes and channels. Of course, new channels and new services are to be welcomed as contributions to the richness and diversity of broadcasting. What has not been so welcome has been both the widening gap between the viewing and listening experiences of different sectors of the population and the extent to which increased competition has resulted in purely commercial considerations becoming the driving forces in the whole broadcasting system.

It is my contention that the important debate is about the future of public service broadcasting ideals in a multi-faith multicultural society. The need to discover and articulate a genuinely public conception of broadcasting has never been more urgent. I believe that Christians ought to be in the forefront of those arguing for a renewal of public service. And as far as religious broadcasting is concerned, I am convinced that if the battle for the public service ideal is lost religious broadcasting will be so marginalised that its value will be negligible.

The recent history of broadcasting is the story of the ways in which both the *public* and the *service* aspects of public service broadcasting have been challenged and weakened. This tendency should, in my view, be vigorously resisted. It has to be resisted for two reasons. The first reason is that genuine public discourse and public debate are vital necessities in maintaining and enhancing the quality of life in our societies. Across Europe we see rising political and socio-economic tensions in countries in which public dialogue and the possibility of common understandings are breaking down. The broadcasting system needs to retain a significant public dimension if it is to be a force for social and cultural cohesion. Christians, who have a faith that has a profound concern for the common good, should be actively engaged in promoting such a public dimension.

Secondly, a society which undervalues the virtue of service to others is a society which hinders the possibilities for human growth and development. It will be a self-centred and selfish society. Broadcasting animated by a selfish spirit will treat the audience simply as consumers of products or as subjects for manipulation and propaganda. Christian respect for the dignity and freedom of the person demands that broadcasting be organized to serve and not exploit the viewer and listener.

Today we need broadcasting which celebrates the richness and complexity of human experience, which respects the dignity and freedom of the viewer or listener and which seeks not only to entertain, but also to inform and educate. In other words we need the ideal of public service to underpin our broadcasting system, whether that system be public or private.

It is sometimes argued that attachment to public service ideals is simply not tenable as we enter an era of multi-channel abundance. Technology and commerce, those twin goddesses of the marketplace, it is asserted, will pull down the pillars of the public temple and set up their stalls in its place. But this future is not inevitable. We have seen in Britain how quickly the replacement of one Prime Minister with another can usher a new political mood and how soon ideological certainties are subject to pragmatic modification. In Europe as a whole there is still a significant political tradition which sees a value in public culture including public broadcasting.

Christians need not despair, therefore, that the public tradition in broadcasting is necessarily doomed. Nor ought they to think that the public service ideal can be found only in publicly-funded broadcasting corporations. Public service broadcasting is above all else an attitude of mind towards the viewing and listening public. As such its survival is not dependent upon particular regulatory practices nor upon modes of finance. Regulations and financial arrangements can help or hinder the expression of the public service ideal but they cannot substitute for it. The ideal of public service will live where broadcasters want it to live; not least in the spirit which animates individual programmes whether or not they are broadcast on so-called public service channels. In Britain, at the moment, there is some evidence that the spirit of public service is more strongly alive in certain commercial television companies than it is in parts of the BBC.

Unfortunately the present spirit of public service does not appeal to all who profess themselves Christian. Public service broadcasters and some Christian groups have found themselves locked in impassioned debates about the nature of religious broadcasting and its future in a more market-oriented broadcasting system. Public service broadcasting has been attacked for failing to give sufficient expression to the passionate convictions of large numbers of Christian believers. Under the guise of neutrality, it is claimed, the public service system operates a covert censorship of views which fall outside the prevailing liberal consensus.

This criticism seems to me to be misplaced. Public service broadcasting exists to serve the interests of the whole community and is obliged to try and reflect the nature of that community if it is to be broadly acceptable. Reith and the pioneers of public broadcasting attempted to build a tradition which would encapsulate a moral vision, a common idea of the good. Radio and television was organized and regulated within a public service framework which, it was hoped, would help to sustain, if not actually build, a sense of national and civic identity based upon generally agreed Christian and moral principles. Reith's original view of the purpose of religious broadcasting was that it should provide the nation with a "thoroughgoing, manly and optimistic" Christian message. But the assumed moral and religious consensus upon which this vision was based has now dissolved and Britain is no longer a Christian nation. It is a society of many faiths in which a minority of people profess allegiance to a religious tradition.

Over the years broadcasters have had to adapt the notion of public service as the nature of the public itself has changed. This change in the audience has meant that broadcasters have had to learn to communicate with people who cannot be presumed to share religious, moral or cultural values. Public service broadcasters have had to respond to changing audience perceptions and tastes by developing a professional ideology based on the virtues of tolerance, objectivity and impartiality which has allowed them to retain a general acceptance among all sections of the public.

In religious broadcasting this ideology finds expression in a desire to create a public forum within which as many different viewpoints as possible are heard and examined. The public service ideal eschews the passionate advocacy of any one particular dogma or creed in favour of what Colin Morris, in his book *Wrestling with an Angel*, has called a "cool examination of every aspect of religion on behalf of a public at once sceptical of its claims and yet intrigued by them".

Of course present-day religious broadcasting in a public service context can be improved. If it is to retain its vigour in the new broadcasting era its scope must be widened. Religious broadcasting must embrace more whole-heartedly the multifaith pluralistic nature of modern society. This means that in the words of the evidence submitted to the Annan Committee on the Future of Broadcasting by the Central Religious Advisory Committee in 1975, "there should be even greater variety; more exposition, more speculation, more experiment. There is a 'climate of religion', inside and outside the Churches, in which the fundamental issues of human purpose and destiny have become matters for probing speculation, rather than for easy affirmation or denial".

Like Colin Morris I believe that the unique contribution which public service religious broadcasting can make is in the provision of a forum in which religious experiences and claims can be held up to a detached, yet not unsympathetic, scrutiny. This kind of broadcasting will be an essential service in an age in which, in his words, "a veritable Babel of ghostly voices will canvass the claims of this or that dogmatism". Morris goes on to say that "public service religious broadcasting...will find itself fulfilling that Pauline role of testing the spirits to see whether they be of God. In other words, religious broadcasting imbued with a public service spirit will keep alive the possibility of a real exchange of views between advocates of different traditions.

If this public forum ideal is to be realised, however, religious broadcasting must be kept alive on national broadcasting networks. Even with a host of new cable and satellite channels the major public and commercial television terrestrial networks will retain the major part of the viewing audience. Because of their presence on public service channels religious programmes can reach substantial audiences. The popular *Thought for the Day* on BBC Radio 4, for example, has a regular audience of 2 million and the Sunday evening television programmes *Highway* and *Songs of Praise* can reach around 14 million people between them. If religious broadcasting is pushed to the margins on such channels it will find it almost impossible to reach the majority of the non-church-going public. The evidence is there to see in the world of radio. Local commercial radio in Britain has now been effectively deregulated and many stations have begun to abandon religious broadcasting. The general audience is unlikely to be reached by specialized religious stations which will mainly reach the already committed.

I believe that public service broadcasting as an ideal is worthy of support from Christians in that it is broadcasting which respects the integrity and dignity of the viewer or listener. The public service ideal also does not draw sharp distinctions between informational, educational and entertaining programmes. It recognizes and attempts to cater for the whole person by providing programmes and channels which range across the spectrum of public tastes and interests.

Critics of public service broadcasting need also to take proper account of the extent to which religious broadcasting is presently subsidized by the broadcasters. In Britain religious broadcasting costs the religious groups very little. Because of the public service ideal religious programming on television and on BBC network radio is entirely financed by the broadcasting companies. Religious groups are having to find money to help finance religious programmes on local radio but this a small amount compared to the millions of pounds spent by the BBC and commercial companies.

The philosophy of public service acknowledges that religion has a central place in human life and thus is an integral part of any general programme output, while market-driven broadcasting recognizes only that religion appeals to a minority audience, like sport, education, and even news and public affairs, which can be catered for by specialist channels. That is why it is worth defending public service broadcasting. Having Christian radio stations or television channels would, to my mind, be a poor substitute.

All of us are viewers and listeners and all of us will be poorer if the public service ideal is allowed to fade.

Dr. Jim McDonnell is Director of the Catholic Communications Centre, London.

XVIII

Pauline Webb

Shall Faith Speak Peace unto Faith?

Communication is of itself an ecumenical word, meaning literally "that which binds together in one". Modern communication technology makes it possible for the whole earth to become one "world-house", the literal meaning of the word *oikoumene*. It thus inevitably overrides many of the barriers that have separated peoples from peoples throughout the centuries-both the natural barriers of ocean and terrain and the more solid barriers of walls and frontiers created by human hands. But deeper and more impenetrable than any of these are the fundamental divisions of the human community based on what is believed to be divine revelation, interpreted through the many different human traditions of faith.

The founding of the British Broadcasting Corporation was at the outset believed by its first Director-General, Sir John Reith, a dour and devoted Scots Presbyterian, to be itself an act of God. Still today in the entrance hall of Broadcasting House is enshrined on a plaque the dedication of the whole enterprise to the glory of God and to the extension of virtue throughout the land. Reith saw broadcasting as a unifying force, giving to rich and poor alike the opportunity of enlarging their life's horizon, and creating a new sense of community across the whole nation.

That included in Reith's view the promulgation of a "dynamic" rather than an institutional Christianity, represented by the inclusion in broadcasting of the best preachers the churches

125

could provide, without giving undue prominence to any one particular Church, despite the fact that both Scotland and England have Churches of established status. He saw broadcasting too as having a reconciling role between the nations, and adopted as the motto for the BBC the Biblical-sounding prophecy, "Nation shall speak peace unto nation".

But if broadcasting were to be a unifying force, what role could religion play in it? Despite the fact that "religion", like "communication" is a word meaning that which binds together, it has proved to be in fact one of the most divisive elements in society. Moreover, with the various religious bodies being concerned to propagate their particular version of the truth, it very easily degenerates into the related word, propaganda, against which a public corporation like the BBC had determinedly set its face. Reith had his own way of meeting these problems.

In carrying out their divinely-ordained vocation, the broadcasters would in Reith's view inevitably have to take seriously the claims of religion to be included both in their practice and in their programmes, but it would be regarded as part of the educational output, intended rather to enlighten the public than to persuade them to any particular way of belief. The BBC Charter of 1927 makes no mention of religion at all, but the following year in the *BBC Handbook*, it was clearly stated that religion must be seen to be an integral part of the stated aim of the BBC to educate, and it was no coincidence that the first Director of Religious Broadcasting was also the first Director of Education. The aim of such broadcasting was enunciated in words notably free of any kind of doctrinal or credal emphasis:

"When those who were responsible for broadcasting set before themselves the object of raising the national standard of values and of a constructive idealism, it was obvious that the religious service should be one of the regular programme features."[24]

From the outset Reith sought the co-operation of all the mainstream denominations in advising on the content of religious broadcasts and selecting the people to take part in them. The first Advisory Committee to be appointed by the BBC was a Religious Advisory Committee which was from the outset even in 1923 fully ecumenical. Its first three members were an Anglican priest, a Presbyterian minister and a Roman Catholic layman and it was rapidly expanded to include representatives of the Nonconformist Churches of Wales and England. But it was not long before the voices of criticism arose from churches like the Seventh Day Adventists and from anti-religious groups like the British Humanist Society, arguing that this was a highly selective group which did not recognise the diversity of religious views in the land. Defending his policy of keeping only to what were called the "mainstream" religious traditions, Reith wrote in his book *Broadcast over Britain*:

"Christianity happens to be the stated and official religion of this country; it is recognised by the Crown. This is a fact that those who have criticised our right to broadcast the Christian religion would do well to bear in mind."[25]

Despite Reith's enthusiasm for religious broadcasting he did not at first receive wholesale approval from the Churches, many of whose leaders regarded it as rivalling their own responsibilities, and were suspicious of what was essentially a secular organisation having control over religious output. In return, Reith himself had little time for the official representatives of the institutional Church and relied instead upon people like the Rev. Dick Sheppard of St Martin in the Fields who professed himself to prefer "a diffused rather than a sectional Christianity".

Early on in the days of religious broadcasting a Daily Service was begun, a custom which has continued ever since, making it the longest-running programme on BBC Radio. From the outset this too was ecumenical, drawing on the hymnody and devotional anthologies of many different denominations, and even developing a liturgical tradition of its own, which was expressed in a special book of prayers drawn from many sources and entitled *New Every Morning*. The *BBC Hymnbook*, published to accompany the services, was one of the first ecumenical hymnbooks to come into general use.

When other outside-broadcast services were planned, a fairly strict tally was kept of the amount of time allocated to the different denominations, which was expected to be proportionate to the numerical strength of their membership. But inevitably this meant that the listeners, and later the viewers, who were not members of the particular Church being broadcast, were treated in effect as eavesdroppers or onlookers at programmes not specifically designed for the medium through which they were transmitted. Moreover, it was insisted that there should not be any kind of proselytising across the denominations nor were the broadcasts allowed to have any sectarian bias, which in some cases became itself an inhibiting factor.

As far as the staffing of religious broadcasting was concerned, professional competence played a greater part in selection than denominational allegiance, so that from the start there was an ecumenical team, including early on at the BBC an ordained woman of the Congregationalist Church working happily alongside brother Anglican clerics. But even in this ecumenical team for many years a special exception had to made in that a Roman Catholic adviser was appointed, with a specific role relating to any programmes originating from or dealing with the Roman Catholic Church.

Throughout the early years of broadcasting this ecumenism was always between Churches rather than between faiths, and religious broadcasting was conceived of as almost exclusively Christian broadcasting. Only after the Second World War, with the steep decline in churchgoing and the arrival in Britain of immigrant communities with strong religious traditions of their own, was it acknowledged that "religious" broadcasting need not necessarily imply exclusively Christian broadcasting, but that other faiths should also be given a hearing, if the religious life of post-war Britain were to be adequately reflected. By 1977, in the revision and re-interpretation of the guidelines governing religious broadcasting, it was explicitly recognised that the principal religious traditions represented in Britain were no longer exclusively Christian.

It was in the World Service of the BBC that this change in the concept of "religious", as distinct from "Christian" broadcasting first became most evident. Throughout the 1970s tentative efforts were made to include in the repertoire of religious programmes a larger number of speakers from other world faiths, and by the 1980s it had become established practice to have a kind of rota of speakers representing the various world faiths on a weekly basis. The rule of thumb was that every Friday, that being the main day for public prayers in the Muslim faith, a Muslim speaker should be invited to give the daily meditation; on Saturdays, the Jewish Sabbath, a Jew would speak; and on Sundays a Christian. The other major faiths would be invited to contribute on one or other of their many great religious festival days.

There were in the early days some elementary errors made, largely due to the unfamiliarity with one another's faiths and to the different attitudes to this kind of presentation of religion on the air. For example, allocating the Sabbath to Jews raised problems, as an Orthodox Jew would use neither a microphone nor a radio on this holy day. That problem was overcome by a careful announcement that these programmes were pre-recorded, and by scheduling which enabled them to be heard after the sun had gone down on the Sabbath. More difficult was the problem of persuading the representatives of the various faiths to present their material in ways that made it comprehensible to those outside their own faith community, for it had to be emphasised that religious broadcasting is not there primarily to provide for the needs of the adherents of the various faiths, but for the public as a whole. Not being used to addressing largely secular audiences this presented a great challenge to imams and rabbis alike. But it also led to the discovery of treasure-stores of legends and parables in all the faith traditions, many of them drawn from the sacred scriptures of the various faiths. It was especially difficult for those faiths whose tradition is not so much verbal but visual and ritualistic to communicate through the sound medium of radio, but they too had their epics and legends and haunting songs to share. But most difficult of all came the same question as had been raised between the denominations. By what criterion is it decided which faiths to include and which to exclude? And even within the major faiths, which particular voices ought to be heard?

The test applied had to be an ecumenical one. Which sects were in fact ecumenical in their attitudes, and would be prepared to accept the restrictions on proselytism and propaganda which must apply in multifaith broadcasting as much as in an exclusively Christian output? And who were the representatives of what could be called the "mainstream"? Inevitably the answer became a selective one and needed constantly to be revised.

But, despite these hurdles, out of our first steps in multifaith broadcasting we moved on into more progressive dialogue, in which we invited representatives of the different faiths to meet together with one another regularly in the context of studio discussion. There we discussed together the meaning of some of the words of faith we have in common but which may have different interpretations within the different communities. By having the same team-a rabbi, a Hindu priest, a Muslim scholar and a Christian theologian, week by week, a rapport was developed between them, which made possible both honest dissent as well as respect for each other's views.

Response to such inter-faith broadcasts has been lively, to say the least, and particularly when prayers from the different traditions are included within the same broadcast. At the time of the recent Gulf War, for example, when the BBC broadcast periods of intercession in which Jewish, Muslim and Christian prayers were all included, reactions varied from outrage to gratitude that at least in tentative ways people of different faiths were hearing each others' prayers even if they were not yet able to pray together. No doubt it will take a long time of profound theological reflection before this kind of sharing across the faiths can be fully accepted. Meanwhile religious broadcasting, if it is true to its name, ought at least to be sowing the seeds of such new ecumenism, and, in a world of such sectarian strife, make it possible for "faith to speak peace unto faith".

Dr. Pauline Webb, writer, lecturer and broadcaster, is a former Organiser of Religious Broadcasting for the BBC World Service.

XIX

Angela Tilby

Television and Evangelism: A Cautionary Note

How effective is television as an evangelistic medium? And what are its limits?

The pros and cons of television evangelism have been put elsewhere. What concerns me is the assumption that those on both sides of the argument make about the medium itself. Both sides regard television as a one-way system of communication with devastating power to intrude on our lives and determine them. This puts programme makers in a position of enormous power. They are the senders of messages which end up inside the heads of the viewers.

Such a picture appeals to those who believe that television is a powerful tool in preaching the gospel. They are awed by its ability to reach into people's homes and believe that it has unique powers to persuade and convert. They believe, without irony, that Jesus would have used television to reach ordinary people just as he preached to vast crowds in Galilee.

On the other hand there are those who argue that it is the overwhelming power of the medium which makes it unsuitable for evangelism. They would claim that television subverts true communication by turning free subjects into screen-sized objects. It by-passes the need for relationship between sender and receiver. It deceives the viewer into mistaking images for reality, it completely misses the transcendence of God and substitutes the true gospel of the word made flesh into the false gospel of the word made image.

Both positions take for granted the immense power of television and its ability to construct and control reality. Depending on your operative theology, it is either the perfect medium for the message of an omnipotent God who works miracles with the precision and directness of a laser beam, or it is a dangerous tool of idolatry which must be shunned by the pure in heart and poor in spirit.

I reject the assumption behind both positions. First, because it reeks of the fear and envy that characterises much Christian response to leisure, pleasure and entertainment; second, because it simply doesn't ring true to my experience as a programme-maker and a viewer. Individual programmes, strands, even channels and networks do not possess that much power to construct or control. Television is a series of mirrors, not a laser beam; a feedback loop out of and into ordinary life and not an autonomous generator of detached, bodiless images.

The programmes that work are not those that seek to drive the Truth into people's skulls, but those which connect, which tell truths which the viewer already knows or is predisposed to know again or in a fresh way. To think otherwise is to make too much of television and to fail to realise how ultimately dependent television itself is on cultural values which, though it may enhance, it does not originate.

By saying this I am not denying that television is transforming our lives in ways that are important for those who seek to spread the gospel. The point at issue is whether television really is one-way communication and therefore to be greeted or shunned as a tool in evangelism.

When I hear people talking casually about what they have seen on television it is obvious that they watch critically. They may look like couch potatoes, but they are not empty, passive recipients of the seductive, flickering images. They assent to and dissent from what they see, and they see what they see through a variety of cultural lenses. A television audience is composed of highly-tuned sensors who are involved in a constant, not always conscious, mental and emotional dialogue with what they see on the screen. Producers like myself do not have total one-way access to an audience. It would be intolerable if we did.

In fact we are often misunderstood. This could be a source of humiliation, more often it is a cause of wonder. Viewers read programmes according to the life-scripts they carry with them. They will frequently see what I did not see or intend; and fail to see what I thought I had designed. They are not alone. I see different things at different times in my own work and in that of others.

As a viewer I can and do attend to television in many different ways. Sometimes I fantasise, flick channels, make a cup of tea or go to sleep. I am often infuriated, sometimes depressed, frightened, amused or delighted. Every programme maker wants to believe that they control the event of a television transmission, that they can send a pristine and perfect image into the air to be received in its totality, but this is a fantasy. A movie being screened in a darkened cinema gets more of a chance, but even if I am enthralled by a show, I do not see precisely the programme that the maker intended. Viewers bring what they are, what their experience not watching television has made them. They bring their own temperament and ailments, their own political prejudices and preferences. These are not created by television. They are created in the flesh by sense experience and relationship, by the thoughts and feelings they already have.

People know when they, or their point of view is not being represented, or when their presence is being distorted or misunderstood, and their dissent feeds back eventually into the attitudes and prejudices of the medium itself. Television becomes a battleground between the status quo and the emerging voices of change. This can work positively or negatively. For example, television makes apparent certain injustices in society. Television demonstrates instances of racism and sexism. It lays them bare by mirroring what is the case. In the early 1950s patronising and even directly disparaging remarks about black people were frequent in documentaries and news bulletins.

Such prejudice, over time, produces protest, even outrage. This takes time to be heard because most of the makers of television at a senior level are male and white.

133

But eventually something gets through. There is a demand for a change in the imagery, and at first it is a bit self-conscious, then it takes over. The mirrors respond and repent and gradually integrate the changes. Eventually (though this may take a very long time) women and black people are appointed to senior positions within television companies. Television can help to heal cultural distortions. It may be slow and piecemeal, but it works.

A negative example. Most people indulge in sexual and violent fantasy from time to time. Large numbers of the same people for various reasons disapprove of fantasies of sex and violence. Television provides some sex and violence; too much for some, not enough for others. Yet it is caught between the desire and the disapproval and will be attacked from both sides. In attacking television on such a matter we are, of course, attacking ourselves and our own ambivalence.

In both examples the mirroring effect of television is clear. In the first example a biased reflection causes protest and change. In the second, television mirrors our own ambivalence, our desire for sex and violence and our refusal to own our desire and deal with it intelligently.

This mirroring effect would not happen if television really did have the power to work like a laser beam, cutting through the mists of prejudice and preference that we bring to it. But it does not have that power. As I have suggested it is more like a feedback loop, through which a diverse society talks to itself.

Within the cultural and moral limits of society this loop is self-correcting. If television is controlled by an intellectual elite there will be pressure for more entertainment. If it is trivial and boring and repetitive there will be pressure for quality. We have seen both these pressures colliding in Western culture in recent years and their collision raises interesting questions of ownership and finance.

It will always be so and if either side is denied for long enough the credibility of the medium will become questionable. People will simply no longer believe what they see. They may go on watching but they will watch with ironic distance. This is what I believe happens when television is used, intentionally or not, as a propaganda tool without due regard for the fact that it is already a two-way medium, a set of mirrors which enhance but do not create the diverse worlds we live in.

Where does evangelism fit into this? The question requires a sophisticated and nuanced understanding of what is happening to Western culture in the 1990s and what the Christian gospel might be beginning to mean within such a culture as ours. One thing we do know is that there are very many people for whom the gospel of Jesus Christ as it is proclaimed today is a matter of indifference. This is a cultural fact, and it is not the consequence of television, though television knows that it is true.

Television has no more power to plant the gospel into this alien soil than the churches and evangelistic organisations have. On the other hand it has no less. But what may be important is to understand why the ground is unreceptive, what it is about our gospel which is so unpersuasive to vast numbers of people.

Until we know this we are bound to project our fantasies of power and control on to television either as enemy or friend. What would be more costly, and perhaps more important, would be to learn to enter the feedback loop of television as bearers and receivers of the hopes and fears of our audiences. That would involve a certain humility which is rare in the Christian world. But without it we remain as sounding brass and clashing cymbal, demanding power where we have failed in charity.

Angela Tilby is a religious producer for BBC Television.

XX

Michael Shoesmith

The Implications of Technological Change[26]

Communication technology is always on a journey, spurred on by commercial pressure and innovation, hindered by inertia and reluctance to buy new equipment, diverted by politicians wishing to control its message. In our childhood, we join the technology at the staging point which it has reached, the place which seems to each of us like the beginning of the whole trip. When I joined, radio was taken for granted. It required no explanation, it just was. I saw only one television set before 1939, so that when post-war television broadcasting resumed in my mid-teens I perceived it as a novelty for the whole human race. Similarly, for my children television was an everlasting fact of life, but home computers were a novelty.

The radio which I remember from my earliest childhood operated on a universal standard. The dial on the bakelite set was inscribed with the names of international towns and cities, and though some of the programmes howled or hissed or were inaccessible for reasons of language, they could all be received with the single technology of our home radio set. I even participated in overseas broadcasting, wearing with pride a silver Ovaltinies badge (not a bronze one, as did lesser mortals) courtesy of the programmes broadcast by Radio Luxembourg. It never occurred to me years later that the 9-inch Murphy television set on which we watched such programmes as *Café Continental* was operating to a standard unique to Britain. And why should the uniqueness matter? We were following the standard used in 1937 when serious television in Britain began, and since television signals had such a short range that there was no obvious possibility of Télévision Luxembourg bringing news of the Ovaltinies with pictures, what did it matter if the French had a different standard, or the Americans?

Radio has been singularly fortunate in operating to a single world standard, and even with later developments it still retains this huge advantage. Frequency-modulated and stereo radio receivers operate internationally, and open-reel audio tape recorders operate at the same group of speeds and with basically only two technical sets of parameters. Other audio-only recording methods have sorted themselves out, courtesy of the market. The Philips audio-cassette overcame and effectively eliminated the cartridge recorder. The Compact Disc is now universal. If Digital Audio Tape recording becomes widespread in the world consumer market, it will be to a single standard.

Other technologies have been less fortunate. Television never had a worldwide standard, partly because in the early days there were advantages in having the frame frequency locked to the mains frequency, so that European systems used 50 cycles per second to lock a system giving 25 frames-per-second, and America (and Japan, then, and possibly for the last time, following the Americans) using 60 cycles per second to lock a 30-frames-per-second picture. As it happened, they also chose to use different numbers of lines in each frame. It is very difficult to break out of this trap, because the high cost of reception equipment has meant that it has been politically unacceptable to produce a new system which renders all existing reception equipment useless.

So the world is still divided between users of 625-line 25-frames-per-second pictures and 525-line 30-frames-per-second pictures. The irony is that because for one good reason no single standard was possible, there has been nothing to prevent chauvinists of many nations insisting on their own pet standard for their national broadcasting. So there are now over a dozen different standards in the world, some differing in only slight respects, but enough to cause problems in communication between nations.

We need to understand that this may not be entirely accidental. It has never been possible to enclose radio broadcasting within national boundaries, but attempts have been made by governments to stop their citizens sharing television from another country. This has been possible because a typical modern television signal requires a bandwidth of 8MHz, though they manage with less in the United States where they need to fit in as many stations as possible. Even if the whole FM band used by public radio broadcasting were used for television, it would provide room only for two television frequencies.

Television must therefore operate on much higher frequency bands than that, and the higher the frequency the more the signal behaves like light, and the less it bends round corners. The curvature of the earth is very useful to the censor who wants to stop his citizens watching programmes from across the border. Further, if the sets are incompatible, only the most enthusiastic will persevere. This made barriers to outsiders very effective for many years. It is hard to believe now, but in the early days of television satellites the government of the USSR said that if a satellite intended for a western European country could be received in their own, they would regard this as an unfriendly act, and therefore by implication that they would feel free to take action to remove the satellite.

On top of this political diversity, there has been added in the field of home video recording a commercial diversity. There have been at least seven different attempts so far at producing a standard recording format, and the war between them is bloody and continuing. The continuation of the battle depends to a large extent on the commercial competition between Sony on one side and the other Japanese manufacturers on the other, a battle which is also taking place with professional video recording standards. The success of the different formats in different markets has a great deal to do with marketing strengths and less with technical quality or rational planning.

Whereas the world of radio planning and development is comparatively sedate, the technological revolution in which we are now involved with television and video is a world of cowboys and Indians, with a lot of people trying to shoot each other very dead. There is a great deal of money at stake for channel operators and for hardware manufacturers. We join this running battle at an interesting point, as most groups have now identified their targets. For the electronics industry, the goal is HDTV, High-Definition Television on a large, wide screen. For the new breed of non-traditional broadcasters, the goal is maximum unrestricted access to homes.

The battle over the MAC standard is an important skirmish. MAC has many advantages over the existing methods of broadcasting colour pictures, which are similar to each other, and were ingeniously devised to be receivable in black and white on black and white sets. The NTSC/PAL/SECAM system broadcast the colour information (chrominance) as a kind of descant above the melody of the brightness (luminance). The smart colour set listens for the descant and uses it, the black-and- white set cannot hear it. Unfortunately, sometimes the descant goes too low, or the melody goes too high, and the set mistakes one for the other. You can see this happen most clearly when a man in a finely-patterned suit appears on colour television, and amazing moire patterns appear.

As the MAC concept is important but baffling to many people, I shall risk an analogy. Imagine you are trying to communicate a piece of music to an organist so that he may play it as he hears it. You choose to send it so that he may listen to it through headphones. In the PAL/SECAM systems, the audio, the notes he will play on the pedals, is of a quite different frequency, so he has no difficulty in picking this out. We have already seen that the melody and the descant (representing brightness and colour), which he will need to play on two different manuals, are usually easy to distinguish, but sometimes get muddled because they overlap.

The equivalent of the MAC principle becomes possible if the organist has a good memory, and can play one line while listening to the next. If he can remember a line of music at a time, it would be easy enough to whistle the tune faster than he could play it, say at twice the normal speed. That would give plenty of time to whistle the descant for the same line of music immediately afterwards. In fact, because for technical reasons it is not so important for the descant (colour) to be note perfect, it would be possible to whistle it even faster, and still leave some time over.

And that is when you could send the pedal line (audio). But as the pedal line is much simpler than the melody or descant, why not speak the names of the notes? That would be so fast that there would be time to speak anything else you chose, say the score of a football match. If the organist had a phenomenal memory, he would then be able to play perfectly the next line of melody with the descant and the pedal notes. After a while, he would also know the day's football results.

That phenomenal memory has its equivalent in the world of electronics, and it is this which makes the MAC system a possibility. The brightness signal for each line is sent at double speed, the colour information even faster, and the sound sent as a packet of digits. Two of its principal benefits are that it gives better picture reproduction by separating the brightness and colour signals, and that by packaging the sound neatly (and digitally) into the flow of picture information which has a wide-bandwidth it allows for the possibility of fitting a lot of other things in as well.

Television engineers are becoming very familiar with the idea of fitting other things in. For example, work is going on at the moment to find room in the terrestrial broadcasting system for many desirable extra features, and they are running out of room. They include a device for removing "ghost" images, the provision of a running-commentary track for people with visual handicap, and even a specially-adjusted audio for people with hearing problems. By contrast with PAL and SECAM, the MAC system allows a lot of room for extras. The D-MAC system has no problems with eight different high-quality audio tracks and a good deal of data as well. The D2-MAC system which at the moment seems the most likely to become a European standard can offer half as much (the only difference is that the digits run at half the speed).

Further, the MAC system allows a step-by-step approach to the television grail, High Definition Television. An easy way to define this concept is to say that it offers a picture large enough and clear enough for you not to notice much difference if it were made even larger and even clearer. It turns out that as far as transmission standards are concerned, we do not have to travel as far as might be supposed. If we were roughly to double the number of lines and double the number of images each second, and at the same time make the picture image rather wider so that it looks like a wide-screen cinema screen, we should have achieved the aim. It would not feel like Cinerama, or offer stereoscopic pictures, or produce the clarity of a projected colour slide, but tests show that it would satisfy most people.

Inventive television engineers, manufacturers of television equipment, film-lovers, and - who knows? - the general public, would love it. The Japanese have invented and manufactured a system called Hi-Vision, which offers it now, at a price. But it suffers from the extreme disadvantage that no present-day receiver would receive anything useful from a Hi-Vision transmission, and it is thought that this might make people cross. It also suffers from the political disadvantage of being a nail in the coffin of the European electronics industry.

By contrast, MAC is European (developed by the Independent Broadcasting Authority in Britain), and a simple MAC receiver can easily be made to receive a sensible picture from a High-Definition MAC transmission. There is therefore a lot to be said for encouraging people to acquire the MAC decoder which is the start of this process. This became possible when satellite broadcasting began.

Satellites for television transmission sit 20,000 miles up in the sky over the equator, circling the earth once every 24 hours, and so appearing to stand still to us, standing on our rotating earth (as the hammer must appear still to the hammer-thrower, spinning round at an athletics meeting). They broadcast at colossally high frequencies a small spotlight of radio beam, its strongest signal marking out a footprint on the earth only a few hundred miles across. Receiving the tiny signal (the transponder relies on electricity from solar panels, and operates at about the power of an electric-light bulb) requires the familiar dish and in front of it an amplifier which hugely increases its strength and also changes its frequency to a much lower and more manageable one. This then goes by cable to the satellite receiver, which amplifies it further, and selects the signal by tuning it. It transforms the signal into the PAL or SECAM system which the ordinary television set then accepts, or better it sends separate colour and audio signals direct to the output of the television set, by-passing the PAL and SECAM circuits altogether.

MAC therefore became very interesting when satellites were planned for direct-to-home broadcasting. People were going to have to buy a satellite receiver. It would cost in principle very little for a MAC decoder chip to be inserted at the end of the receiver circuit, and so at no disadvantage to anybody and with considerable improvement in the picture and audio quality the first small step would be taken along the road to High-Definition Television.

In fact, it became so interesting that the European Broadcasting Union committed itself to using one or other of the MAC systems for all direct-to-home satellite broadcasting. At the World Radio Administrative Conference in 1977, satellite positions and frequencies had been allocated on a country-by-country basis (although few probably thought that the channels for Iceland and Vatican City, for example, would be rapidly taken up). At that time, it was envisaged that the broadcasts would be in NTSC/PAL/SECAM. It was something of an achievement therefore to persuade the EBU to commit to using the MAC system, and unfortunately the political price which was paid was that it could be any MAC system, not one in particular. The position was formalised in a directive of the European Commission in 1986.

Then two other things happened which changed history. First, it took a lot longer to make the MAC chips than had been expected. Second, it became possible to receive pictures at home from communication satellites, lower power satellites broadcasting on a different range of frequencies which were originally intended to send telephone traffic, to provide feeds to cable stations or for broadcasters to use to share programmes. The rules about using MAC which the European Commission had laid down did not apply to these satellites, and in particular to the Astra satellite. Britain saw the biggest battle in this field. Sky Broadcasting began an energetic campaign to persuade the British public to watch programmes using PAL from the Astra satellite, while BSB followed the European Commission rules and waited and waited for receiving sets to be available to watch D-MAC programmes from Marcopolo. In the end, as we now know, they waited too long.

The rules of the European Commission Directive were due to be revised in 1991, and a draft directive was to be presented to the Council of Ministers in June 1991, which was expected to make D2-MAC the future European satellite standard. In the event, it was not possible to come to a common mind amongst all the parties involved, and the issue had to be postponed. However, the technology Commisssioner announced large subsidies to encourage future use of D2-MAC.

One day, it will no doubt become simple to have a dish which will swivel to point at any satellite in the sky, and which will decode whatever system is being used for broadcasting and offer signals to the television set in a form which it can accept. Now, it is expensive. It is therefore very attractive to offer many programmes from one point in the sky (no moving of the dish) and using one coding system (no complication with decoder chips). Astra now offers 32 channels, which will almost certainly increase to 48. Although the broadcasts can be in any standard, it seems likely that most will be in PAL for the present.

The positions of the satellites are described by the lines of longitude on which they stand at the Equator. Astra is at 19 degrees East. At 19 degrees West, there is a group of satellites which follow the European Commission rules (more or less!). They are TDF 1, the French national satellite; TV-Sat 2, the German national satellite (TV-Sat 1 having failed technically); Olympus, the satellite of the European Space Agency also broadcast from there until it was lost. They are in a 75-kilometre box in the sky, but to us tiny mortals 20,000 miles away they appear to be in the same place.

To this same box it is expected that there will be added in 1996 (possibly even in 1993) Europesat, which is the direct-to-home satellite project of the people behind Eutelsat (which is a range of satellites similar to Astra). Nine European countries (but not including Britain) have requested between them 39 transponders on Europesat. If this all happens, and if Astra continues, there will in the long term be at least two significant "hot-spots" in the sky over Europe.

In June 1991 there were 17 satellites, in a total of 14 different positions, which could be watched in Britain alone. Between them, they were broadcasting over 100 different channels. 25 of them were examples of what the trade calls "double-illumination", when the same channel can be received from several different satellites (sometimes in different colour coding - PAL, SECAM, D2-MAC). If all the channels now planned for the future are taken up, it is very difficult to know where all the programmes will come from.

To some, this is a great virtue. All may tell their story, if they can find a hearer. Satellite television services also offer broadcasting room for radio channels, some of them digital. There are over 60 such radio services now broadcasting in Europe. The problem here is a cultural one of persuading radio listeners that they could listen through their hi-fi to programmes which have reached their home through a satellite television receiver. One British attempt to use a channel for Christian radio broadcasting was strikingly unsuccessful.

Meanwhile, in the United States, a huge amount of time and money has been invested in High Definition Digital Television. It began for commercial reasons, as a battle by American engineers and manufacturers to defeat the Japanese attempt to have Hi-Vision adopted as a world standard. Up to 1990, it seemed that digital television was too far away to be worth waiting for, and that there would be a generation's use for HDTV using MAC or something similar, with digital sound but analogue pictures. Now astonishing results have been achieved in solving a number of problems to do with the huge, impossibly large, bandwidth which digital wide-screen television ought to require. The moment you start using digits, you move into the world of computers, and they are becoming smarter and smarter. Storing pictures in digital form is just like storing digits in a computer, using the same technology. Two techniques are used to reduce the amount that has to be sent. One is to send only an update signal from one frame of picture to the next, transmitting only those parts of the picture which have changed. The other is a mathematical trick of compressing a great deal of the information before sending it. The Americans are convinced that the problems of putting this into practice have now been licked. Five groups have put forward proposals for a HDTV system for terrestrial broadcasting in the United States, and four of those are digital.

The FCC will consider the results of tests of these systems in June 1992, and choose the system to be used in the spring of 1993. If it works on the limited bandwidth of terrestrial systems, it will be wonderful on the wider bandwidth possible with satellite. It makes no attempt whatever to be compatible with existing American sets. All HDTV broadcasting would be on separate channels, and additional to existing transmissions. The FCC does not regulate the technology of satellite or cable distribution, though it would seem likely that broadcasters would want to use this same system, if it works.

And at the same time in Europe a lot of work is going on to improve PAL in various ways, so that it can overcome some of the deficiencies which led to MAC's development in the first place, and so that it can be extended to offer wide-screen as an option. At the moment, however, it seems likely that it is HD-MAC which will become the European standard for wide-screen broadcasting.

So much for the vain hope that we would be able in the next generation to move to a universal world standard for television. However, it is clear that one day we shall have digital television, certainly within fifteen years, probably within ten, and some would say within five. When we do, the standards become less important, because once we have a collection of digits in a frame store to deal with, the job of reading them out and putting them through whatever receiving apparatus we happen to possess is comparatively straightforward. Curiously, the most expensive part of a High Definition Television system is likely to be the picture display, the cathode ray tube or its successor. And that is the oldest technology in the television set.

For the moment, however, multi standards present major problems in acquiring audiences. In addition to the barriers already mentioned, many satellite channels, for reasons of cost-recovery or copyright enforcement, are encrypted. There are several methods of doing this, mostly based on the idea of line-rotation. In this method, the line of picture is not sent intact. It is divided into two parts, and the second is sent first. The receiver puts them back together the right way round, because it knows where the two parts join - which varies from line to line. How it knows depends on which encryption system is used.

It is very difficult to cheat with the later systems, but a substantial market built up in pirate equipment to unscramble some of the earlier systems. The intention now is that the Eurocrypt system of encryption should become the European standard, though BSkyB uses two completely different systems on Marcopolo and Astra. At least seven different encryption systems are currently in use in Europe.

There has to be an easier way to receive the programmes than this! It is, of course, cable. Let the cable operator cope with the encryption, the copyright, the subscription, the standards, the dishes, the changes which take place almost weekly in who is broadcasting what from where. While older cable systems have a problem in that their copper wires can only carry a limited number of programmes, modern systems use thin glass filaments along which pass laser-light, bouncing its way from a central source to a box at the corner of your road. The laser-light can be modulated with a very large number of different frequencies, and even more since it has turned out that two different colours of light can be used, and the huge capacity doubled. So the box at the corner of the road has access if necessary to more channels than any home is likely to want to see, and each home can be connected to it by a length of coaxial cable (though one day it seems likely that it will be fibre-optics all the way). The cable operator can regulate which channels you can see, and is therefore able to charge for the use of particular channels, or even for individual programmes.

Cable offers not only great variety but also the possibility of interactivity. Indeed, in Britain it is the ability to offer the interactive telephone line rather than the one-way programme delivery which has attracted the (mostly American) companies to provide a widespread cable service at what will be a cost of over £4 billion. In principle, there are more interactive possibilities in a cable system than simply a telephone line. Cable and satellite can be seen in one way as alternative delivery systems for the same channels, to be used respectively by town and country dwellers. Christians who rate interactivity in communication as important may find themselves prejudiced in favour of the potential of modern cable systems, although experiments in a limited form of interactivity through audio- conferencing have been a feature of some of the experiments in the Eurostep channel on Olympus, which relied on direct broadcasting.

There is no such thing as a free broadcasting channel. There is a clear financial transaction involved in cable delivery, which is rented. Some satellite-delivered channels are funded by advertising, or more truthfully hope to be. Of these, some offer general entertainment, but many specialise, for example in sport or popular music, or in two cases in news. Some are national broadcasts, delivered by satellite for convenience, particularly as a supplementary service in countries which have problems with terrestrial transmission. Some are attempts to export national culture, by countries willing to finance this. Some are film channels, funded by a subscription through cable or directly by a charge for providing the key to the encryption system. There are two views as to whether the broadcasting service owes the cable operator money for providing an audience and hence an enlarged advertising revenue (as in Germany), or whether the cable operator owes the broadcasting service money for providing the programmes which justify the cable rental.

Several important themes can be observed. The first is redundancy. Old technology was fully used. On my typewriter, there may have been one or two keys which I never struck, but they would have been very few. On my computer there are hundreds of facilities which I have not used, and never shall. No matter. Let the Protestant ethic drop away. It is still worth having my computer for what it does, and I do not need to justify the parts I never use. It is altogether more like the human brain, which has massive redundancy built into it. The stroke victim who learns to speak again is grateful for it. Modern communication technologies offer redundancy which offends those of us who were brought up with one single national television channel, which spoke to us like the unique word of God. "It must be true," we said, "I saw it on the television."

Now an absurd number of channels offer absurd programmes, often from more than one transmitter. Old third-rate American movies are endlessly recycled, dubbed into different languages. Games are played for public entertainment which would be tedious to play in person at a party. Pornography with no pretence to artistic merit appears, evidently as a kind of night-cap for those who need some sexual encouragement. What a waste! But a waste of what? Nobody is compelled to watch. It would only be disastrous if it made it impossible for other programmes to be broadcast. In fact, redundancy makes it more possible for other programmes to be broadcast. If we do not like what we see, and do not see what we would like, there is a remedy in our own hands.

The second theme is convergence. It is the digits which have done it. My word processor; the technology of electronic mail, by which I can communicate with you through our computers; the fax machine, which carries an image by wire; the compact disc, which provides near perfect sound-reproduction; teletext pages on the television screen; soon, the television and radio programmes themselves. They all rely on a stream of digits, which can be processed and stored in similar ways, which can be sent down copper wires or optical fibres, or broadcast from a satellite. Interchangeability between them all is theoretically possible now, and practically likely in the not too distant future.

The third theme is interactivity. At its lowest level, it is the ability to choose much more widely, to construct an evening's viewing so that if you want to see sport you are not locked into a film, and vice versa. This also includes time-shift viewing through home video recorders. But it also offers the option of making programmes of your own with camcorders which produce pictures only marginally less good than those delivered by the professionals (and better than some cable and satellite pictures at the point of delivery).

What we do not yet see clearly is the way to put it all together so that a free market can build up in programmes, and a potential listener or viewer can discover what is available, use it, contribute to its cost, and interact with the person who made it. Just give us a little more time.

Michael Shoesmith is now based in Birmingham. He directs Skopos which offers Christian education and training programmes by satellite television.

XXI

Derek C. Weber

Making Graven Images

"Have you ever thought about the fact that two of the first three commandments really have to do with communication about God? ... Think about it. 'Thou shalt not take the name of the Lord in vain:' - one should speak only in certain ways about the Lord - and 'Thou shalt not make any graven images.' The commandment about graven images interests me the most because graven images are concrete images of God. And God is never to be made into a concrete image, but is only to be known through the Word and in the Word." (Neil Postman[27])

In the midst of all the excitement over the possibilities television provides we need to take a moment to examine the whole process of religious communication. What are we trying to do when we put the gospel on the television screen? And, more importantly, what happens to the message when we embrace this medium? While I do not want to throw out the baby with the bath water, when it comes to Christian television broadcasting, I would at least like us to admit that the bath water is murky enough to make the baby hard to see. The two commandments mentioned by Neil Postman provide a framework for questioning the enterprise we call Christian broadcasting.

THOU SHALT NOT TAKE THE NAME OF THE LORD IN VAIN

How are we to speak about God? This question searches the theological nature of communication. What is the function of communication? What role does it play in human community? "Communication is the fundamental human fact... The essence of our humanity lies in this fact." So said Roger Mehl. Communication implies a relationship: there must be sender and receiver. For there to be any type of relationship, any point of contact between persons there must be communication. This does not necessarily require language, for communication can be on other levels than the purely verbal. But it does require communication. Theologian Henrik Kraemer names this relationship-building function of communication as "communication between."[28]

The partner of "communication between" is "communication of". This is the message-relaying function. However, says Kraemer, while a distinction can be made between these two functions, there can be no complete separation. Therefore, the goal of communication could be said to be both conveying messages and creating community; community being defined as the sphere in which human relationships are created and maintained.

In community persons exercise their relationships through communication, as both sender and receiver. "Communication between" implies reciprocity as well as a recognition of individual worth. The question then arises, does television subvert this process? The "sender" is quite removed from the "receiver", therefore it is hard to recognize relationship-building at work. Communities created through these types of communication would not be communities based on human relationships, but upon information mediated one-way. Television seems to have disposed of "communication between" for the sake of more efficient "communication of."

Yet, there is talk of "television communities" or the "global village", meaning that through television people are brought together in a shared experience. Can we now legitimately speak of a "mediated community" in which individuals in front of their screens are indeed bound together by the message? In some ways this seems true. A common starting point for many conversations is a recap of a programme or news item: Did you see so-and-so? An answer in the affirmative begins a relationship that might have no other grounds for contact. Isolated individuals can take part in a shared experience; rejoicing at their team's success in the World Cup hundreds of miles away; sitting in reverential silence during a royal wedding or as a new archbishop is enthroned; sharing in a nation's grief through a televised memorial service after a great disaster. A community is created through media. But is it a community of a different sort? Is it a community that is missing something fundamental? A million people laugh at the same joke, yet they laugh in their ones and twos. Does not the Christian gospel call for a community that is more than disembodied voices in the loneliness?

If the first question we must ask is a general one about the theology of communication, the second is a specific question about content. In other words, how can the Christian message be communicated? Is this a message that can be communicated along with the myriad of other messages to be communicated in an information-saturated society? Or is there some fundamental difference to this message that requires a specific approach to its communication? Are there methods of communicating this message that would be inappropriate; that would deny the message even as it tries to speak the message?

It is the task of the communicator to use the most appropriate media possible to communicate the message. The communicator's task according to F. W. Dillistone is "to determine what are the most significant instruments for conveying information to our modern world and what are the language forms which have the widest currency in ordinary speech."[29] Writing his *Christianity and Communication* thirty years ago, Dillistone already began to suspect the vast impact that television was going to have. It is obvious that the language forms with the widest currency at least in the West, if not the world as a whole, can be found in television.

Yet, in addition to considering whether television created the most common language forms, we must also ask with Ronald Falconer whether these forms are the most appropriate vocabulary available. It is not the ubiquity of the influence of television, but the appropriateness we must question. If television has difficulty fulfilling the "communication-between" requirement necessary for a Christian understanding of communication, ought we not disregard such methods of communication in communicating the Christian message? This is indeed a pertinent question that must be debated if the Church is to continue using television to communicate. Does the technology of television prevent a true communication of the gospel? In *Message, Media and Mission* Ronald Falconer expresses grave doubts about the appropriateness of television.[30] "There is something about the nature of television which makes events larger than life, thus distorting the truth about them". Malcolm Muggeridge also was concerned. "Our amazing technology has a built-in *reductio ad absurdam*, whereas the Word that became flesh and dwelt among us full of grace and truth, in the most literal sense, speaks for itself."[31]

It is the technology of camera and screen, of microphone and receiver that separates speaker and hearer, that redirects attention from the real to the fantasy, from the important to the trivial. The whole television environment might be one where the Christian gospel, no matter how well it was presented, would be swallowed up by the overriding message of television.

That message is a powerful one. At present it is the media, led by television, that ask what it means to be human. The answers provided vary from suggesting that *meaning* comes from *owning*, to the idea that the good life is wrapped up in youth and beauty. Television must first re-interpret personal needs, notably religious needs for meaning and a sense of worth and belonging, into material needs to own and to be accepted in a material culture.

"That television is effective in creating common belief patterns is demonstrated by research. Studies show consistently that heavy viewers of television begin to reflect the perceptions and myths which television subtly propagates. They also suggest that the messages of television bypass critical mental faculties and are absorbed impressionistically within the subconscious. The challenge which this massive alternate belief system, which is being worshipped for $4\frac{1}{2}$ months of 12-hour days each year by most Australians, poses for traditional religious faith has yet to be taken seriously by scholars and educators." (Peter Horsfield.[32])

In addition, some would argue that the normal pattern for television-viewing, regardless of the content, may not be conducive to religious or spiritual awareness. For many people television functions as a source for relaxation, a space where no demands are made on the intellect. It is true that most people in Western Europe look to television as the main source for information. However, they also look for it to be structured in fairly simple ways; packaged, as Postman would say, as entertainment.

Another area of concern is in the realm of imagination. Exercises in imagination are integral to the life of faith and an understanding of theology. Television, some believe, negates the use of imagination. Television provides the pictures and leaves little for the imagination to do. Many studies of the development of children indicate that while television is good for some forms of play, primarily re-enactment, it reduces the level of imaginative play. It is precisely this argument that is raised by Neil Postman.

Thou Shalt Not Make any Graven Images

What of religion-on-television? It is often said that what is generally perceived to be missing from most of television's output is any concept of the transcendent; any idea that there is something, anything, beyond the flickering images on the screen. A major problem here is that of focus. Television needs something upon which to focus: a person, place or thing that the camera or microphone or transmitter can pick up. This means that the concrete and the specific broadcast much more clearly than the spiritual. Therefore there is a lack of reference-to or recognition-of a world beyond the one in which we live day to day. The gospel, the image and Word of Christ is more difficult to put on the screen. In the attempts that are made something is invariably lost. At times it is the message of the gospel itself that is lost as the focus shifts to the preacher or expert. As Postman reminds us, people say, "I don't know about God, but Jimmy Swaggart I can see. He sings to me and he prays and he asks me to do things. There is his image right in front of me."

At other times it is the subjectivity that is lost, the idea that the discussion on the screen has anything to do with the viewer. Dr.

Chris Arthur says that "while the aim of many media presentations may be to impart information about religion, the aim of religion itself is not information but redemptive transformation".

It is precisely this subjectivity that defines the gospel. This is the issue with which long before the age of television Søren Kierkegaard wrestled in *Training in Christianity*.[33] He contrasted direct communication with indirect communication. It is, he argued, indirect communication that invites the hearer to respond, to believe, to engage. This is the method adopted by Christ himself. It is the method of the Word. As Postman rightly says:

"All I know is that there is tremendous importance in the vagueness of language. The great thing about the Bible ... is that [it is] vague in the important parts. That permits people, as time passes, to infuse these words with new and more appropriate meanings. That keeps the documents living. In other words, the very vagueness and ambiguity of these writings permit people to see things in new ways and allow new ideas to come into our culture."[34]

Television on the other hand, deals with direct communication, with specific reference points and visual images that lock ideas in place. Zeffirelli's *Jesus of Nazareth* points out one of the problems. The visual images in the film become more definitive, more interpretive than word-images. Jesus, for many people, bears a striking resemblance to Robert Powell. Visual images can limit the freedom to discover truth. Direct communication is more than merely inadequate, it is a distortion of the truth. The truth is distorted because the subjective is objectified. The subjective involvement in the message is left out, as is the possibility for choice and also the possibility for a true response in faith; which by definition must allow for the possibility for disbelief.

Speaking on the future of broadcasting at Edinburgh University in 1990, Pauline Webb referred to this process of objectifying a subjective reality. Despite the entry of cameras and microphones into churches, "We can never expect that technological communication can replace that much deeper communication that takes place only within the gathered community, when we communicate together with one another and with God at the table of the Lord. So, the communication of religious faith can never be regarded as simply a marketable commodity. To take this creative word, intended as an expression in human form of the love of God and sell it to the market of the mass media can be as much a form of prostitution as offering any kind of love for sale".

These are strong words of warning. But are they words of prohibition? That, I believe, has yet to be completely decided. However, the dangers are plentiful and the benefits somewhat unclear. We have that verse from Matthew urging us to tell the world, we have the capabilities for global transmission, we have committed men and women working in the field. Still we must ask: what is happening to the message as it is translated to the screen?

Derek Weber is Project Officer of the Media and Theological Education Project at New College, University of Edinburgh. He is a minister of the United Methodist Church of the U.S.A.

XXII

Ingmar Lindqvist

It Depends. . .

Does Christian outreach mean that the Churches should use satellite TV? I'm prepared to say that it depends.

Let's think back to the very first Christmas Eve. Here are the shepherds. There is a young woman in labour. Up in the sky is a host of angels. The shepherds got the message. They went. They saw. They were conquered; lost in the bottomless depths of a child's wide-open eyes. Turning back and praising God they had become the first believers in the Christ-child.

So far so good. But if God is almighty, why did he not inform all of mankind of his will and intentions? He could have staged a global communications network increasing the number of angels at will. Eventually they would have surrounded the whole world. Why on earth did God settle on a tiny little baby that took thirty years to grow up into a not very imposing figure? After thirty years the man went to work - for three years. Most of that time He spent in the company of twelve men. Most of the rest of the time He devoted to individuals. What a waste.

Why on earth did He not call in the angels? He could have reached all of His contemporaries within an instant. The angels could have sung Gospel songs all over the land. Fantastic quality. Fantastic rhythm. Fantastic robes. Fantastic outreach. But no. He just kept roaming the Palestinian countryside; healing and saving one man here and another woman there on His way to Golgotha.

A waste of time? Stupidity? Or could it be that God knew his communication theory long before anybody else even dreamt of such a thing?

If you have something very important to say - like "I love you" -and you very badly want to make an impact, be sure to be there in person! Take it from me. Or from God. Or from communication theory.

Our product as Christians and as Christian Churches is wrapped in face-to-face communication. Without face-to-face communication we have no faith-communication. We have lost the Gospel. So let's do whatever we can to increase communication on a person-to-person basis.

That's my way of looking at the role of the media in the life of Christians and Christian churches. But NO! It's not that easy. There *was* a host of angels, wasn't there? The audience was rather a small crowd but the singing was angelic all the same and it bore the distinct marks of firsthand knowledge, of sharing a secret. As a result the shepherds did not start commenting on fantastic musical scores nor talk about the great gospel night in the shepherds' field. Nor did the angels ask these shepherds who were longing for salvation to raise their hands or to come forward and kneel in prayer. The angelic choir made way for personal encounters. But without the angelic heralds how could they have known there was something for them to see?

The shepherds went because their curiosity had been aroused, their innermost longings nourished. That's why they saw him - the Messiah - face-to-face. Let the media be the media. Let the media be means to an end, choirs of angels, means to promote personal communication. Christians and churches cannot do without mass media. But if we never get past the media to the point of facing each other we may as well close our churches and congregational halls and use their bulletin boards to keep passers-by informed of so-called Christian programmes in the media.

So it depends. It depends on whether we use the media, acknowledging that we are in the advertisement business. If so, then I'm all for using the media as much as we can and as well as we can. But I have to disagree with those who, when they have made something on television, think they are presenting people with the real thing.

But another story altogether is that God may even use advertisements to save a lost sheep - in spite of communication theory. To me certain mass media products may be legitimately labelled "Christian" if they point away from themselves, if they are Go-and-see-for-yourselves programmes - Philip-programmes.

Still another story is the use churches could make of media when concentrating on the sheep who are *within* the fold.

Ingmar Lindqvist belongs to Finland's Swedish-speaking minority. As well as being a television producer, Dr. Lindqvist is a film-maker, philosopher and communications theorist.

XXIII

David M. Adams

Two Cheers for Freedom

I confess to a cautious welcome for the new freedoms now emerging in broadcasting across Europe. Change is always uncomfortable and some traditions will undoubtedly die, but what develops could be more vibrant and dynamic and it is this which fuels my hopes.

The changes provide an opportunity to re-design the way religious broadcasting works. Christians can now use local cable television to serve their needs in community building and they can also make programmes for the public channels. There may, it seems to me, also be space for a third development - a new kind of "public service" television.

Budget cuts on most of the existing channels are already affecting the religious output. Commercial competition is likely to provide an excuse to marginalise religion further. There will be less opportunity to explore the religious horizon. The best religious journalists may drift into other departments. This in itself may not be a bad thing. I have always thought that religious values were just as important in drama and current affairs as in worship. What is clear is that religion served up by an articulate liberal establishment cannot satisfy the new wave of spiritual life now sweeping the churches. Most people want something more down to earth.

The new freedoms are particularly welcome to those outside the mainstream. Many of these groups see the gospel as a message to be delivered and television as their platform. In point of fact, an evangelical faith fits television well. The medium willingly serves those with clear, unambiguous conviction.

But there are pitfalls to be avoided. Television can, in the words of Neil Postman, rob the gospel of all that is historic, human and holy. Christian television is not public relations for Jesus. We already have on record the sad experience of those who considered the medium to be neutral and who assumed that it was only its content which needed changing. Their experience however taught us that the richness of faith is easily trivialised and the integrity of faith easily compromised. The medium distorted the message and the sacred was profaned.

The message of Christ has been more than information ever since the Word became flesh. Christian communication flows out of life and in particular the shared experience of faith. It is the fruit of our contemplation in community. Christ made it clear that our community relationships authenticate our claims both for Him and for ourselves. We need to give careful attention not only to our words but also to our (His) body language.

These messages arise in the smaller groups in which we live. This is where we must begin our media plans. These local communities of faith are repeatedly re-telling "the old, old story of Jesus and his love" in their own way. When these stories walk successfully between yesterday's idiom and today's fashion with freshness and faithfulness we come close to finding the source of Christian communication. Surely it is here that we can expect the transcendent to come down to earth, today.

For the most part this activity will be small and local. Community television, delivered by cable or even video, needs to be something the community plays with and uses in its ordinary life together. Here its value as an interactive instrument will develop a new understanding of its accountability - often the missing element in larger broadcasting systems. In this process its participants can become TV-articulate, learning its language as producers and not just as consumers.

At times the journalistic and technical standards may be poor and some fear the tyranny of the worst. But this is simply an electronic version of the newspaper industry. Problems do arise when a group becomes too ambitious and tries to reach the world simply because the technology suggests the possibility. Christian groups who buy their way onto commercial channels are, it seems to me, in danger of making this mistake.

So at one end of the spectrum lies community-based television. At the other, there remains the public service system. The recent American campus debate on ethnicity and the curriculum raises the prospect, in that society, of the end of a shared culture. The omen is disturbing. I agree with Jonathan Sacks that without common values society will sink into tribalism. European public broadcasting has provided a canopy of public culture during the turbulence of twentieth-century pluralism and this tradition must be maintained. Commercial competition will make its future more difficult, but it must not be allowed to destroy it. If public service broadcasting is not to become simply the choice of the elite, its attraction must remain broad. Here entertainment can still be re-creation and religion can still provoke and inspire.

Changes in the approach to religion will certainly be necessary. Public television must learn how to accommodate those outside the liberal mainstream. The thresholds will need to be re-examined. Faith isn't always rational or articulate. It isn't just an issue to debate or a phenomenon to describe. It cannot be fully explored without allowing it to propagate. This will mean that the public broadcasters must come alongside religious life not only to reflect its activities but also to give its representatives the open space to make programmes themselves.

But the conditions for participation in public broadcasting cannot be dictated by the churches in the way they can set the standards in the private sector. To qualify for involvement we must learn the rules of public discourse and attend to the public agenda.

Christians will always be found in the "naked public square" and their stories will from time to time provoke the kind of questions to which the gospel is the answer. At times their intervention is lateral - coming alongside unobtrusively, like Christ on the road to Emmaus, to offer points of reference which are important to the interpretation of life's experience. Occasionally it can be confrontational, like Balaam's donkey, stopping life in its tracks and pushing the listener to the boundary of the familiar, where truth may be found.

There is, then, a place in religious broadcasting for private initiative to serve the communication needs of Christian communities and there is a need to maintain religion on public television. But if, as it seems, "you and your cause do not exist unless you are on television", it is legitimate to ask whether an active community system and a limited public service presence can fully represent Christian faith.

The answer is no. There seems to be space left for the development of a third stream, a system which reflects the unity and diversity which is Christ's body on earth and which celebrates its contribution to western culture and social life - Christian "public service" broadcasting if you will. Its programming could be deemed in the public interest, after all, to follow Brunner, the church is the only institution which exists for the benefit of its non-members. At the same time it could serve to sustain and promote the values and views of this unique "city of faith". It was Christ who first spoke of a city set on a hill.

Obviously the Church is not a broadcaster and it would be wrong to assign this activity to her communication officers. But a broad, controlled-access channel could be organised along similar lines to public service. Responsibility would need to be vested in a board of governors chosen to represent its "public". Programme policy would need to create space for the diversity to be expressed and to allow the different traditions to weave a colourful tapestry of faith. Where differences exist these issues could be explored for the common good and our shared values will shape both the ethos and substance of the output. With cameras and microphones set up at the intersections of the city to capture her conversations this service could offer a Christian perspective on the wider issues of contemporary life.

The model is not entirely new. VISN, the multi-faith channel in the USA (which embraces groups within the Judaeo-Christian tradition) and the religious sector of EUROSTEP (the pan-European satellite channel where 4 different Christian groups co-exist) are exploring the way. The result is more than a common carrier - it is an ecumenical instrument in the making.

We are on the edge of a new Europe. Of all our institutions, it is the church whose history runs longest and whose influence runs deepest. Perhaps the new structures of broadcasting can serve this awakening *oikumene*.

I readily admit that this model will require courage and re-straint, and the virtues of tolerance and fair play. I doubt that these proposals can become the whole of religious broadcasting. Some groups will take the easier commercial path. But perhaps these ideas can be a part of the future, even if, just now, they are no more than a mustard seed.

David Adams is European director of Trans World Radio. He is based in Hilversum.

XXIV

Carlos A. Valle

Three Cheers for Community

Communication is a gift of God to humankind. Communication is essential for the human being. Moreover the human being is communication. I become a human being if I can communicate with others. There is no humanity in isolation. Without a "you" a human being cannot exist (M. Buber). In the same way there is no Church without "others" Our communication with God is always a communication about our neighbour.

Communication is an act of participation. Participation is the action through which God is working out the creation of a community developed on the basis of concern for the helpless.

The good news to which the Holy Spirit witnesses is that, over against everything which is a sign of death, God in Jesus Christ has said Yes to life and has done so in a decisive liberating act, beginning with the dispossessed.

From this perspective, Christian communication is nothing less than participating in God's action. God creates community in Jesus Christ, in an act of proclamation and denunciation, so that life will grow in dialogue, creativity and integration of the community.

The nucleus of our faith is intimately related to what happened in the first century. But what took place then did not come to an end. Biblical witness says that what occurred at that time and place has produced a dynamic movement that is recreated in each encounter on a personal and social level.

Christian communication therefore has to do not with a "closed" content, complete in itself, but with a present, active God. Christian communicators do not hold a copyright on the Gospel - which is not a property to be possessed but a living reality.

To communicate this living reality the churches are called to be communicating communities. This means that they *are* communicating not only through their words and actions, but also by their ecclesiastical structures, the architecture of their temples, their music, the liturgical vestments, their political involvement and also through their silences, absences and much more.

One crucial question is how are the people perceiving this communication?

What are the elements that shape or distort that communication? What is the distance between what the churches think they are communicating and what the people are really receiving? Today we have the means at our disposal which can help us gain an understanding of the true meaning of our communication that goes beyond our communicating words.

Communication is not confined to a better use of old or new tools to establish our communication. Today communication is helping us, for example, to understand the way in which human beings relate to each other: the potential and the limitations of the instruments we use: the capability of these instruments for producing meanings beyond our intention.

But communication is teaching us to understand that we need to talk of a total communication. We cannot confine our communication to the transmission of words. The purity of our doctrine doesn't prevent people from receiving a communication that contradicts the essence of the Christian message.

Sometimes, for example, the churches have ignored the importance of feelings. Highly developed audio-visual media are persistently exciting our senses, appealing to our feelings. It is true that this type of appeal makes us much more vulnerable than a rational approach: but it cannot be ignored or rejected because it is essential to our human nature.

Communication can help us to go beyond theological rationalisations to let us appreciate the *importance of pictures and sounds*. Here the Orthodox tradition has a very important contribution to make. In *Icons, Windows on Eternity*[35] Gennadios Limouris has compiled several important contributions on communication. He affirms that "Icons and other forms of art are instruments of prayer and, as such, as important as the preaching of the Word of God", because he thinks that "through the lines, forms, expressions and colours they announce the Good News of the Gospel and open new horizons for Christ's message to penetrate all parts of the world". It is possible that some people find it difficult to accept this affirmation. Nevertheless, it speaks about the manifold forms in which a church can manifest itself as a communicating community.

All this helps us to understand the very close relationship between *culture* and *communication* which leads us to a fairer appraisal of the cultural roots of our people and communities.

It gives an incentive to appreciate our traditions, rediscover values, treasures of the past in a new perspective.

But also it helps us to look from a new perspective at the long missionary tradition of many churches. The desire, for example, to introduce the faith into a particular culture, apparently gave the missionary enterprises the idea that their own culture was similar (or identical?) to the Gospel, and that both their culture and the Gospel were universal.

It is interesting to notice how that idea was accepted in different places without - apparently - raising any questions. Some Latin American preachers even have the foreign accent that the missionaries necessarily acquired in their effort to speak the native language: or have become used, in torrid regions, to wearing dark, warm clothes, brought by the missionaries from their frigid homelands.

But these are only signs of deeper things. On the one side we have the imposition of a culture as if it were a supreme gift identified with the Gospel, thus, of a sacred character. On the other hand, we have disdain and destruction, with a total disregard for the diverse cultures which the missionaries aimed to reach. In this way, and in the name of unity, certain missionary enterprises did away with a wealth of local contributions: many ancestral traditions were censured as sinful, and they created a stereotyped image of what a human being should be.

All this brings us to the incredible world of modern technology that attracts many Christians so much. Some are so dazzled by the possibilities that technology offers that, in many places, it has become the new idol capable of solving all our problems. And technology does not belong to just one national or racial group; nor can it be identified with one particular political or economic system. It cannot be considered from an ethical point of view. It is in a class of its own, that of benefactor, provider of well-being and progress. However, in spite of how much we value technology in our world, we must remember that this image is rather naive and tends to make us forget that it does not exist independently of the political and economic world and that, sometimes, it is a direct product of that world.

Faced with this situation it would be senseless of us to propose what Babin called "the leap backwards". The solution is not to flee technology, but to start placing it in an ethical context. It is essential to know how technology is affecting the way in which people feel and think.

At the same time we need to learn how technology and the media can become instruments of change. We need to accept that in the modern world media and information are basic tools of communication.

Perhaps we need to conclude with Pierre Babin, when he affirms: "....technology is the privileged place of the Incarnation. Formerly, when one spoke of incarnation, one referred to nation, country and culture. Today, one must speak of technology because the electronic technologies are shaping the new type of person and creating a world where national frontiers are disintegrating. I believe that technologies now constitute the greatest challenge and opportunity for the Incarnation."[36]

Finally I would like to offer a concrete series of signs which can help us to approach our communication and lead to its evaluation.

a) The sender is not the owner of the truth. It is not communication from owners to clients. Both the sender and the perceiver (not the receiver) need to be addressed by the message.

b) Communication promotes dialogue. Dialogue means to speak *and* to listen, to be able to give the word *and* to receive the word from others. These are signs of humanity. For this reason the sender does not claim to have the last word.

c) Communication rejects sectarianism. Sectarianism is often seen in Christian communication in the fact that the effort is to make the perceiver similar to the sender. His language, his proposals, his claims totally ignore other people's cultures, and he sees his own proposals as the only valid ones.

d) Communication is effected within a community. There is no communicator without a community, for there is no evangelisation without the creation of community. The Christian communicator is a part of the whole community. The needs and problems of the community are his own. He is not outside. He speaks from within the community, not outside or above it.

e) Its themes are not limited. Every human concern is also Christ's concern. It is not a matter of forcing the issue in order to include a formal witness. One can analyse many kinds of Christian communication which, no matter where they start from, always end up with a couple of Bible verses being repeated over and over again, which do not have any meaning for the perceiver and lose their deep sense. The Gospel of Jesus Christ has to do with the whole human life and Christian communication has to make this concern evident.

Carlos Valle is General Secretary of the World Association for Christian Communication, the headquarters of which is in London.

XXV

János Györi

Zakeus Video

One of our most important tasks is making programmes. From the very beginning of Christianity it was the most important task of the Church to inform people about the good news. Today we can also fulfil our mission by broadcasting good news about the gospel and about church-life in a way which makes people curious. I speak from my own experience of this. I used to serve in a very good, enthusiastic and free congregation but the time came when the state couldn't stand my work any more. I was removed to a part of Hungary which at that time was the most undeveloped and persecuted. In my new parish I discovered with surprise that I could have a great effect by showing these programmes - those films that I had made in my former congregation as a record of my work. A great part of the results in the new place were due to the inspiration of these programmes.

On special occasions for children we like making collages. We only collect photos and drawings from secular newspapers and magazines, but these pictures take on a totally new dimension. You can imagine Jesus praying in this way: "I do not ask You to take their thoughts, ideas, methods out of the world but I do ask you to keep them safe from the Evil one." During recent times in Hungary, Christian culture was pushed into the background. It is our task to reveal it again. Everything was dictated by ideology. Now it is really important to broadcast scientific programmes which are free from atheism.

János Sámuel Györi is a pastor of the Lutheran Church of Hungary. Under the Communist regime, his parish work with young people was too successful by far. He was sent to be pastor of the small village of Osagárd. Here he has built up a video ministry which he calls Zakeus Video "because people want to see Jesus".

REFERENCES AND NOTES

[1] This is a revised version of Albert van den Heuvel's keynote address to the first Cranfield Conference in October 1990.

[2] This is a condensed version (by Peter Elvy) of a lecture delivered by Jaan Kiivit to a meeting organised by the Church of Finland in Mariehamn, Åland Islands in May, 1991. Translation of the German text by Constanze Lux-Clarke.

[3] "Public Service Broadcasting in Different Cultures", *Communication Research Trends*, Vol. 8, 1987, Nos 3 & 4.

[4] "The Origins of Public Service Broadcasting in Britain", *Communication Research Trends*, Vol. 8, 1987, Nos. 3 & 4, p.6.

[5] Wolfe, Kenneth M, *The Churches and the British Broadcasting Corporation 1922-1956: The Politics of Broadcast Religion*, SCM Press, London, 1984.

[6] Briggs, Asa, *The BBC: The First Fifty Years*, Oxford University Press, 1985.

[7] "Citizens and Consumers: Religious Broadcasting Between Public Service and Deregulation", *Communication Research Trends*, Vol. 8, 1987, Nos 3 & 4, p.17

[8] "The Implications of Deregulation for Religious Broadcasting", *Communication Research Trends*, Vol. 8, 1987, Nos 3 & 4, p.23.

[9] "Cues from the Television", *America*, March 15th, 1988.

[10] "The Great Hunger".

[11] The issue had not been resolved as this book was prepared.

[12] The Co-Production Connection is the title of the Hilversum-based international agency which promotes co-operation and

co-production in Christian broadcasting. It was established by Wim Koole on behalf of the European Ecumenical Satellite Committee.

[13]This conference was organised by the World Association for Christian Communication (WACC) and the Lutheran World Federation (LWF) and was held in Hilversum in May 1991.

[14]Head, Sydney W., *Broadcasting in America: A Survey of Electronic Media*. Houghton Mifflin, Boston, 1990: pp.419-20.

[15]Sterling, Christopher H. and Kittross, John M., *Stay Tuned: A Concise History of American Broadcasting*, 2nd ed., 1990, Wadsworth, Belmont, California, pp.304-5.

[16]Head, p.490

[17]Head, Sydney W., *World Broadcasting Systems: A Comparative Analysis*, 1985, Wadsworth, Belmont, California, pp.74-5.

[18]Head, pp.342-3.

[19]Shegog, Eric, "Religion and Media Imperialism: A European Model", in Ableman, Robert, and Hoover, Stewart M., *Religious Television: Controversies and Conclusions*, 1990, Ablex, Norwood, New Jersey, p.345.

[20]Ibid, p.345.

[21]Quicke, Andrew, "Pressure Group: The Campaign for Independent Religious Broadcasting". In press 1991.

[22]Shegog, p.349.

[23]Ewing, Keith, "British Groups Research Satellite News Service", *Evangelical World*, June 1991, p.3.

[24]*BBC Handbook 1928*, p.131.

[25]Reith, J.W., *Broadcast over Britain*, Hodder and Stoughton, 1924, p.192.

[26]For a more detailed survey, see *Modern Television Systems* by Jim Slater published by Pitman, 1991.

[27]Postman, Neil, "The Door Interview", *The Door*, Nov/Dec 1989, No 108, p.36.

[28]Kraemer, H, *The Communication of the Christian Faith*, Lutterworth Press, London, 1957.

[29]Dillistone, F. W., *Christianity and Communication*, Collins, London, 1956.

[30]Falconer, R., *Message, Media and Mission*, St. Andrew's Press, Edinburgh, 1977.

[31]Muggeridge, Malcolm, *Christ and Media*, Hodder and Stoughton, London, 1987.

[32]Horsfield, Peter, "Religious Dimensions of Television's Uses and Content", *Colloquium*, Vol. 17 No 2, 1985.

[33]Kierkegaard, S, *Training in Christianity*, trans. W. Lowrie, Oxford University Press, 1941.

[34]Webb, Pauline, "Theological and Ethical Reflections, The Future of Broadcasting", Centre for Theology and Public Issues, Edinburgh, 1991 (published proceedings of a conference of the same title held 24 November 1990).

[35]Limouris, Gennadios, *Icons, Windows on Eternity*, World Council of Churches, 1990.

[36]Babin, Pierre, *The New Era in Religious Communication*, Fortress Press, Minneapolis, 1991, p.17.

The Future of Christian Broadcasting in Europe by Peter Elvy, the background document for the first Cranfield Conference was published for the Jerusalem Trust by McCrimmons in 1990.

CONTRIBUTORS

Stephen Abarbanell is in charge of the German Evangelical Church's department of Radio, Television and Film at GEP *(Gemeinshaftswerk der Evangelischen Publizistik)* in Frankfurt am Main.

David Adams is European director of Trans World Radio. He is based in Hilversum.

David W. Clark is Dean of the College of Communication and the Arts of Regent University, Virginia Beach. Since 1977, he has been associated with CBN, the Christian Broadcasting Network founded by the Television Evangelist Pat Robertson. Dr. Clark is now the President of National Religious Broadcasters (NRB).

Brendan Comiskey is Bishop of Ferns in southeast Ireland and has been President of the Catholic Communications Institute of Ireland and Chairman of the Episcopal Commission for Communications since 1982.

Peter Elvy is a consultant to the Jerusalem Trust.

John P. Foley. The Most Reverend John Foley is an American and is the titular Archbishop of Neapolis. Archbishop Foley is the President of the Pontifical Council for Social Communications, Rome.

Duncan B. Forrester is Director of the Centre for Theology and Public Issues, University of Edinburgh

János Sámuel Györi is Lutheran pastor of the village of Osagárd, Hungary where he founded *Zakeus Video.*

Albert H. van den Heuvel has held major offices in the World Council of Churches as well as in Dutch politics. Dr. van den Heuvel is minister-emeritus of the Netherlands Reformed Church and is now vice-Chairman of the Board of the Dutch Broadcasting Corporation.

Jaan Kiivit is a pastor of the Estonian Evangelical Lutheran Church. His parish is in the Estonian capital Tallinn. His late father (also named Jaan Kiivit) was Archbishop of Tallinn.

Wim Koole was director of *IKON*, the Dutch religious programme production house. He now coordinates the Hilversum-based Co-Production Connection, which is sponsored by the European Ecumenical Satellite Committee.

Ingmar Lindqvist belongs to Finland's Swedish-speaking minority. As well as being a television producer, Dr. Lindqvist is a philosopher and communications theorist.

László Lukács was appointed director of the Media Centre for the Hungarian Catholic Bishop's Conference in 1984. Dr. Lukács has published more than two hundred articles and edited several books.

Renato Maiocchi works as a Television producer with the *Federazione delle Chiese Evangeliche in Italia*. He became Chief Producer in 1988. He is a Baptist lay preacher.

Horst Marquardt worked as a radio-journalist in the former Soviet-occupied zone of Germany. A Communist, he found Christ while reading the Bible. In 1960 he felt called to establish *Evangeliums-Rundfunk* in Wetzlar.

Jim McDonnell is Director of the Catholic Communications Centre, London.

Gabriel Nissim joined the Dominican Order in 1954. He produced religious programmes at Radio-Douala, Cameroon and later served as Dominican Novice Master of the province of Paris. He is President and artistic producer of the French Sunday programme *Le jour du seigneur*.

Anthony Pragnell was Deputy Director General of the Independent Broadcasting Authority, London, until 1983

Eric Shegog is Director of Communications of the General Synod of the Church of England.

Michael Shoesmith is now based in Birmingham. He directs *Skopos* which offers Christian education and training programmes by satellite television.

Bill Thatcher is Executive Director of the International Christian Media Commission which has its headquarters in Seattle.

Angela Tilby is a religious producer for BBC Television.

Bob Towler is Commissioning Editor, Religion, at Channel 4, London.

Carlos Valle is General Secretary of the World Association for Christian Communication the headquarters of which is in London.

Pauline Webb is a writer, lecturer and broadcaster and a noted leader of the Methodist Church. Dr. Webb is a former Organiser of Religious Broadcasting, BBC World Service.

Derek Weber is Project Officer of the Media and Theological Education Project at New College, University of Edinburgh. He is a minister of the United Methodist Church of the U.S.A

Nils-Gøran Wetterberg is responsible for all matters concerning radio, film and TV in the Church of Sweden.